BEGINNER'S GUIDE TO JUICING

KICKSTART YOUR JOURNEY AND IN DAYS
EXPERIENCE ENHANCED ENERGY RESTFUL SLEEP
SHARPER FOCUS & BOOST WEIGHT LOSS

JADE JUICE

© **Copyright 2023 - All rights reserved.**

The content contained within this book may not be reproduced, duplicated or transmitted without direct written permission from the author or the publisher.

Under no circumstances will any blame or legal responsibility be held against the publisher, or author, for any damages, reparation, or monetary loss due to the information contained within this book, either directly or indirectly.

Legal Notice:

This book is copyright protected. It is only for personal use. You cannot amend, distribute, sell, use, quote or paraphrase any part, or the content within this book, without the consent of the author or publisher.

Disclaimer Notice:

Please note the information contained within this document is for educational and entertainment purposes only. All effort has been executed to present accurate, up to date, reliable, complete information. No warranties of any kind are declared or implied. Readers acknowledge that the author is not engaged in the rendering of legal, financial, medical or professional advice. The content within this book has been derived from various sources. Please consult a licensed professional before attempting any techniques outlined in this book.

By reading this document, the reader agrees that under no circumstances is the author responsible for any losses, direct or indirect, that are incurred as a result of the use of the information contained within this document, including, but not limited to, errors, omissions, or inaccuracies.

CONTENTS

Introduction   5

1. ALL ABOUT JUICING   11
   - What is Juicing?   12
   - The Basics and Benefits of Juicing   13
   - Interactive Element: Testimonials   14
   - Why Consider Juicing?   15
   - Juicing vs. Blending   17
   - Getting Started   19
   - Pros and Cons of Different Juicers   22

2. MEET YOUR FRUITS AND VEGGIES   25
   - Organic or Conventional   26
   - Organic vs. Natural   28
   - How to Balance Organic and Conventional   30
   - Understanding Your Fruits and Vegetables   33
   - What To Do With the Pulp   38
   - Key Takeaways   44

3. MAKING IT WORK   47
   - Juicing Tips and Hacks: Planning   48
   - Preparation   52
   - Correctly Storing Juice   56
   - Storing Fruits and Veggies   58
   - Setting Goals   60
   - Interactive Element: Goal Setting   63
   - Tips and Strategies for Juicy Goals: 64
   - Key Takeaways   66

4. YOUR SHORT-, MEDIUM-, AND LONG-TERM DETOX PLANS   71
   - What Is a Juice Cleanse?   72
   - Getting Ready for Your Detox   74
   - Prepping for the Ultimate Cleanse   76

Preparing for Your Three-, Five-, or Seven-Day Juice Feast	77
A Three-Day Detox	78
Testimonial: MaeLynn d'Evreux	82
Five-Day Feast	84
Seven-Day Feast	85
Setting Expectations	87
Why You Should Set Expectations	89
Eight- to Fourteen-Day Juice Feast: Professional Juice Feasters Only	91
Navigating the Epic: A 15- to 21-Day Detox/Juice Cleanse	93
Key Takeaways	95
5. JUICING RECIPES FOR YOUR NEEDS	**101**
Digestion and Gut Health	103
Energy	114
Detox	126
Inflammation	135
Sinus	142
Cold and Flu	150
Diabetes	158
Weight Loss	170
Pre- and Post-Workout	182
Conclusion	193
References	201

INTRODUCTION

Hey there, fellow juicy adventurer!

So, guess what? I used to turn my nose up at juicing. I mean, seriously, who slurps down veggies and calls it a meal? Plus, I thought that drinking my fruits and vegetables was a lazy way to avoid chewing and a surefire way to spike my blood sugar levels.

But after a week-long juice cleanse, boy, did I change my tune. Not only did I feel like I had rocket fuel in my veins, but I also dropped a cool 10 pounds. Not too shabby, right?

Are you feeling a bit sluggish or stuck in a rut? Are you fed up with those energy-draining sodas or heart-racing coffees? Are you dreaming of unmasking that inner superhero just waiting to burst forth? If any of these questions got you nodding, then buddy, you've stumbled upon the right book! It's time you join the juicing revolution. Ready for the juicy low-down? Juicing isn't some magic elixir or ancient secret.

Juicing is just the goodness of nature bottled up. This way of life involves consuming fresh juices made from nothing but plants—either as a supplement to your regular meals or as a replacement for some (or all) of them. By following this lifestyle, you can enhance your emotional, psychological, and physical well-being in so many ways.

But wait, there's more! Drinking these vibrant blends might transform you into a lean, green, radiating machine.

Some perks? Check out the following examples (Blackwood, 2023):

- **Shed those pesky pounds (bye-bye, love handles):** It's like having a personal salad chef in your stomach! These low-cal, high-fiber wonders will fill you up faster than a Netflix binge.
- **Light up your energy levels (who knew you could feel this good?):** Fresh juices are the ultimate energy boosters, like your very own power plant. They've got antioxidants, minerals, and nutrients that'll turn you into the Energizer Bunny—batteries not included!
- **Make your skin and hair shine (watch out, sun):** Think of vegetables and fruits as your beauty

squad, armed with antioxidant shields to fend off free radical villains. They'll keep your skin and hair looking so good you'll be mistaken for a Hollywood star.

- **Bolster your immunity (take that, cold season):** Imagine vegetables and fruits as the dynamic duo of your immune system, armed with vitamins and minerals that turn your body into a fortress. Bad germs? More like scared germs!
- **Calm down your body's inflammation and pain (making you feel less like a pin cushion):** Juices are like the ultimate bouncers at the *Inflammation Nightclub*. They spot inflammation trying to sneak in, and with a firm, "You're not on the list, guy," they kick it out, leaving you pain-free and ready to boogie to the rhythm of life.
- **Relax your veins and arteries (scraping off the gunk):** Fruits and veggies are the culinary ninjas, stealthily sneaking into your meals to lower blood pressure and cholesterol.
- **Control your sugar highs and lows (teaching your cells to share):** Think of juices as the wise traffic cops of your bloodstream, ensuring your blood sugar flows smoothly and your insulin sensitivity stays on the straight and narrow—so there are no sugar-induced traffic jams.
- **Scrub your internal organs (say goodbye to those nasty toxins):** Juices waltz in with their detoxifying cocktails and leave your organs

feeling so refreshed that they might just start humming a little detox tune.
- **Enhance your digestion (making your poop slide out):** Fruits and veg are the fiber wizards of the kitchen, performing digestive magic tricks. They turn food into smooth, swift exits from your body, making you the undisputed champion of bathroom races.
- **Cheer you up and make you smarter (who doesn't like being in a good mood?):** Veggies and fruits are like your brain's personal stand-up comedians. They deliver punchlines of essential vitamins and minerals, leaving your mood elevated and your brain sharper than a pineapple slicer.
- **Save you from chronic illness (giving them a good smackdown):** Juices are like the Avengers of nutrition, assembling to protect you from the supervillains of chronic diseases. With them on your side, you're practically invincible.

…and oh so much more.

Just when you thought it couldn't get cooler—juicing is like a spa day for your insides! Think of it as a gentle hug for your colon, flushing out the nasties that could lead to all sorts of health troubles.

Feeling skeptical? Sound a bit like a sci-fi movie? Good news my friend: Science is on team juice! Some studies even suggest juicing can kick-start processes in our body that help keep our insides squeaky clean (Henning, 2017). Think of it like your body's spring cleaning but without the dust and sneezing. It's a natural way to detox and rejuvenate your digestive system. And who doesn't want a happy colon?

In the delightfully juicy pages of this book, you're about to embark on a full-fledged expedition. First, we'll dive headfirst into the juicing essentials, arming you with foundational knowledge, demystifying various juicers, and sharing priceless tips to ensure a silky-smooth experience.

Then, we'll stroll through the vibrant world of fruits and veggies, unveiling the secrets to selecting, prepping, and blending them while savoring their unique flavors.

We'll make juicing an effortless part of your daily routine with inventive approaches. And let's not forget about the detox journey—we'll navigate through detailed three-day, five-day, and seven-day plans, boosted by mouthwatering juice recipes to kickstart your rejuvenation.

To top it off, a diverse treasury of juicing recipes awaits, personalized to meet your health aspirations, whether it's shedding those extra pounds, supercharging your energy levels, or embracing overall wellness.

Now, who am I to guide you on this journey? Just someone who's walked in your shoes! A while back, I was a hot mess—battling health issues and feeling like a drained battery. Then juicing swooped in like a knight in shining armor, and boy, it changed *everything*. Moving to North Dakota led me to a vibrant farmer's market.

My husband and I became plant-based living documentary binge-watchers. That's where juicing came in. At first, our juice experiments were less than stellar, but we stuck with it. We learned the juicing ropes and got a juicer—it was a game-changer.

Morning energy soared, replacing our coffee fix. As active people—me running and him weightlifting—juicing skyrocketed our vitality and helped with weight management. Ours naturally evolved into a 100% plant-based lifestyle, which we still embrace. Now, juicing is a simple and tasty part of our morning routine.

I've been a die-hard juicing fan for 15 years, sharing this magic with others and witnessing their transformations. This book? It's your juicing compass! You'll uncover the science, the how-tos, and even some lip-smacking recipes that'll make your taste buds do the happy dance.

I've poured my years of juicy wisdom into these pages—consider it your handy guide to the juicing universe. So, ready to jump on this juicy wagon? Let's get blending, shake off those toxins, and let your inner glow take center stage.

Cheers to a juicier, zestier you!

1

ALL ABOUT JUICING

Well, if you told me I'd be hopping on the juicing wagon 15 years ago, I'd have laughed—probably while chomping down on a greasy burger or guzzling down a soda. Fruits and veggies? They were just the colorful hurdles I maneuvered around on my plate while my true love was junk food.

But then life decided to slap some sense into me with a health scare that screamed, "Hey, it's time to wise up and take care of yourself!" So, I hopped on the juice train. I embarked on this juicing odyssey, armed with my very first juicer (that didn't break the bank) and a pile of fresh produce. It was like I'd become a mad scientist in my kitchen, whipping up weird concoctions and crossing my fingers.

Guess what? I didn't hate the taste of these liquid experiments. They were shockingly refreshing, energizing, and, dare I say it—surprisingly satisfying. My mood was on the upswing, my energy levels soared, and my skin decided it wanted to glow brighter than a supernova. From that point on, I was hooked. Juicing became my daily ritual, and I was venturing into the uncharted territory of everything plant-based.

Who knew that juicing would be like the spark that set off a fireworks display in my world of healthy eating? I waved goodbye to my old habits of mindlessly munching on junk food and stumbled headfirst into the delightful realm of sipping on fresh produce.

WHAT IS JUICING?

Juicing is like the magical art of extracting the very essence of fresh fruits and veggies. It's a bit like a science experiment in your kitchen, usually involving a nifty machine. But why, you ask? Well, juicing is the secret handshake to getting an intense dose of nutrients, antioxidants, and those fancy phytochemicals found in plants.

There are two main methods of juicing (Brown, 2019):

1. Centrifugal (the speed demons of the juicing world)
2. Cold-press (the Zen masters who love taking their time)

By now, you might be wondering why folks juice. Well, their reasons are as diverse as a fruit basket. Some juice for the health benefits—boosting the immune system, detoxifying, warding off or tackling illnesses, or just packing in more plant goodness.

Others might be on the juicing train for weight loss. These folks want to shed those extra pounds, amp up their metabolism, or treat their colon to a rejuvenating retreat. I'm one of those who juice just for the sheer delight of tasting different flavor combos and experimenting with fresh juice recipes. Juicing is a multi-purpose tool in the toolbox of green, holistic living.

THE BASICS AND BENEFITS OF JUICING

Juicing can provide a concentrated source of nutrients, antioxidants, and phytochemicals from plants and increase the intake of fruits and vegetables for people who do not consume enough of them (Henning, 2017).

Plus, it's the ultimate trick for folks lagging in the "eat your fruits and veggies" game. Juicing can also enhance the absorption of some nutrients by removing the fiber that may interfere with digestion.

Juicing can benefit anyone who wants to improve their health and well-being by consuming more fresh fruits and vegetables. However, juicing is not a substitute for eating whole fruits and vegetables, as it does not provide the same amount of fiber, which is essential for digestive health and satiety. Juicing should be done in moderation and as part of a balanced diet that includes other food groups.

So, before you grab that juicer, it's wise to consult with your doctor or a nutrition expert. They can help you figure out if juicing is safe and suitable for you. They can also help you plan a juicing regimen that meets your nutritional needs and preferences. Remember, with great juicing power comes great responsibility!

INTERACTIVE ELEMENT: TESTIMONIALS

Here are some stories from real people just like me who have benefited from juicing (*Case studies,* n.d.):

- Clark (not Mr. Kent) felt like Superman after doing a five-day juice cleanse. He savored the refreshing juices that nourished his body and mind. He also swore by the ginger shots, which banished his chest infection like a magic spell. He vowed to keep up the shots and repeat the cleanse in the new year.
- Jill found relief from her Crohn's Disease through juicing. She started with ginger shots every morning to soothe her inflamed gut and joints. She grew to love the spicy kick of ginger and its anti-inflammatory effects. She added other juices

to her regimen, guided by her doctor, who knew which ingredients had healing properties and tasted great. She made her own juices at home, but her doctor used a cold-pressed machine that extracted more nutrients. She enjoyed juicing for its health benefits and delicious flavors. She also liked that she could customize her juices, cleanses, and other drinks.
- Carly experienced many health benefits from juicing. She shed some pounds and said goodbye to her hay fever symptoms. She also discovered a quick and easy way to give her kids the daily nutrients they needed by juicing. She was a type 1 diabetic and had to monitor her sugar intake. She did a juice cleanse recently and was amazed that she could halve her insulin dose. This process showed that the natural sugars were easier to digest and required less insulin.

WHY CONSIDER JUICING?

Let's debunk some juicing myths and shed some light on the facts, shall we? In recent years, juicing has become quite the sensation, with folks raving about its health benefits. But within this juicing frenzy, myths have sprouted like overgrown weeds potentially leading people down the wrong path to well-being. I aim to peel back the layers of the most common juicing myths and give you a more comprehensive scoop on the real deal.

Here are some common myths and facts about juicing (Kennedy, 2022):

Myth 1 (fiber gets the boot in juicing):

Fact: Juicing does remove some of the fiber from fruits and veggies, but hold on—it doesn't ditch all of it. Fiber comes in two flavors: "soluble and insoluble." Juicing does trim down the insoluble kind (the one that doesn't play nice with water). But fear not; soluble fiber (the friendly, water-soluble one) remains intact in your juice. This distinction matters because soluble fiber is essential for gut health. It helps with water absorption and keeps your digestive system running smoothly.

Myth 2 (sugar overload in juices):

Fact: The sugar content in your juice depends on the fruits and veggies you use. Fruits like apples and oranges bring a natural sweetness to the party, while veggies like carrots and celery are sugar-saving champs. Worried about sugar? Craft your own concoctions using low-sugar fruits and veggies—take control of your sweet destiny!

Myth 3 (the mythical juice detox):

Fact: "Juice detox" or "cleanse" ideas often raise eyebrows. Remember, your body is a detox dynamo with built-in mechanisms. But certain foods can lend a helping hand. Veggies like broccoli and cauliflower contain goodies that turbocharge your liver's detox game. Sipping juice from these champions can support your body's natural detox process.

Myth 4 (juicing lacks proven health perks):

Fact: Hold on to your juicers—research is starting to back up the benefits. Beet juice can dial down blood pressure and amp up your exercise stamina. Carrot juice might even reduce DNA damage in the white blood cells of smokers. So, the science is sipping right alongside you.

Myth 5 (juices starve you of protein):

Fact: Juices aren't protein powerhouses, that's true. But they make up for it with a buffet of other nutrients like vitamins, minerals, and antioxidants. Craving protein? Some veggies like peas, spinach, and kale are high in protein.

JUICING VS. BLENDING

Juicing and blending are two different ways of processing fruits and vegetables into liquid form. Both have pros and cons, depending on your health goals and preferences.

- **Juicing 101:** When it comes to juicing, the name of the game is extracting pure juice from fruits and vegetables, leaving the pulp and fiber behind. This process results in a potent elixir of vitamins and nutrients, easily assimilated by your body. However, juicing does bid farewell to some valuable compounds, like antioxidants that cozy up with fiber.

- **Blending 101:** On the other side of the blender, we have pureeing whole fruits and veggies, keeping their fiber and pulp intact. This concoction is more filling and satisfying, thanks to fiber's role in regulating digestion and appetite. Fiber also moonlights as a guardian against heart disease, obesity, and diabetes, doing a tap dance on your blood sugar and cholesterol levels. Blending also keeps a tight grip on those antioxidants found in the fibrous nooks and crannies of produce.

Both juicing and blending boost fruit and veggie intake, each with unique perks. However, neither replaces a diverse, balanced diet (Schaefer, 2018):

- **Nutrient concentration:** Juicing offers a nutrient punch per ounce, while blending provides a broader nutrient spectrum.
- **Fiber content:** Juicing strips fiber while blending retains it, aiding digestion and heart health.
- **Antioxidants:** Juice and pulp harbor antioxidants, but some people prefer one camp.
- **Digestion:** Juicing is gentler but can lead to tummy troubles if overdone. Blending might challenge some folks but benefits gut health.

- **Sugar:** Juices may spike blood sugar; blending moderates it, promoting stability.

Juicing and blending each has its unique role in your health journey. Juicing is your go-to for concentrated nutrients in a petite package while blending shines when you crave the fiber and antioxidants in a larger sip.

Both powerhouses help you amp up your fruit and veggie intake with their respective health benefits. Remember, though, neither can replace the magic of a balanced diet that embraces a variety of whole foods.

GETTING STARTED

Juicing seemed like a mountain of work and a waste pile to me. I was clueless about what fruits and vegetables to pick, how to slice them, or how to scrub the juicer.

I was terrified of throwing away money and time on something I hated. But then, I saw a video of a friend creating a delicious juice with just a handful of ingredients. She said it was a breeze and a blast and made her feel amazing. She inspired me to take the plunge.

I bought a simple juicer and some fresh produce from the market. I followed her recipe and made my first juice. It was a carrot-apple-ginger juice that had a sweet and spicy taste. It was heavenly!

I felt a wave of energy and wellness after drinking it. I felt like I was nourishing my body and my soul. I was hooked. I discovered that juicing can be as easy as pie and smooth as silk. And it can be delightful and satisfying.

There are a few sailors you'll need to add to your ship's crew before embarking on your journey (Galea, 2023):

1. **Juicer (your juicing CEO):** The juicer itself is the MVP of your juicing squad. Slow juicers like the Tribest Slowstar Juicer, the Kuvings C7000, or the Tribest Greenstar Elite are like the Zen masters of juicing—they keep those precious nutrients and enzymes intact. Fast juicers? Well, they're a bit like the impatient toddler version of juicers.
2. **Jugs and containers (the catchers of juice and pulp):** Think of these as your trusty catchers—one for the juice and another for the pulp. Most juicers throw these in as a package deal, but if not, make sure they're short enough to slide under those spouts. They're your go-to for pouring, storing, and giving that leftover pulp a new home.
3. **Fruits and vegetables (the star players):** Your A-list ingredients are fresh, organic, and colorful. You can juice almost anything except the dry ones like bananas, avocados, and figs. Spinach, kale, beets, carrots, apples, pears, pineapples, oh my! The more colors you have in your lineup, the more vitamins, minerals, antioxidants, and

phytochemicals you'll score for your health and immunity.

4. **Vegetable brush cleaner (the scrub squad):** Even organic veggies need a good scrub. These brushes enter every nook and cranny, ensuring no dirt or nasties crash your juice party. It's like giving your produce a massage before they dive into the juicer.
5. **Peeler (the quick-change artist):** When fruits and veggies need a wardrobe change (peeling), this tool's got your back. Beets, oranges, grapefruits, pineapples, and melons, we're looking at you! It's quicker and safer than using a knife, so you can make your produce runway-ready.
6. **Knife (slice, dice, and everything nice):** Your trusty sidekick for slicing and dicing. Some veggies need a trim to fit into the juicer's chute, and a sharp knife makes it a breeze. Santoku knives are your best bet. They're versatile and easy to use.
7. **Chopping board (the juicing stage):** The safe, stable platform for your slicing and dicing. Plus, it protects your countertop from scratches and stains. Any chopping board will do, but bamboo cutting boards score points for aesthetics and eco-friendliness.

PROS AND CONS OF DIFFERENT JUICERS

Selecting the perfect juicer is like finding the right sidekick for your juicing quest. There are different types, each with its unique superpowers and quirks.

Here's a quick rundown of the main juicer types (Cassani, 2022):

Centrifugal Juicers (The Speed Demons)

- **Pros:** Affordable and common, they're fast and easy to use.
- **Cons:** They can be noisy party crashers and produce more foam and oxidation. They're not great with leafy greens or wheatgrass.

Masticating Juicers (The Slow and Steady)

- **Pros:** Also known as slow or cold press juicers, they're quieter, produce less foam and oxidation, and excel at juicing leafy greens and wheatgrass. They can make nut butters, sorbets, and baby food.
- **Cons:** They're pricier, slower, and require more cleaning effort than centrifugal juicers.

Twin Gear Juicers (The Juicing Maestros)

- **Pros:** Efficient and effective, they're the kings of juicing. They handle everything from leafy greens to pine needles and extract the highest quality and quantity of juice and nutrients.
- **Cons:** They are pricey, complex, and bulky. Assembling, operating, and cleaning them can feel like tackling a Rubik's Cube.

Citrus/Press Juicers (The Citrus Whisperers)

- **Pros:** Specialized for citrus fruits only, they're simple, inexpensive, and a breeze to use and clean.
- **Cons:** They're one-trick ponies, limited to citrus fruits, and can't juice other produce.

Which juicer is your sidekick? The juicer that suits you best depends on your unique juicing needs and preferences. A centrifugal juicer could be your go-to if you're all about speed, convenience, and budget-friendliness. But if you crave top-notch juice quality and versatility, consider a masticating or twin-gear juicer. Your juicing journey is your choice!

Once upon a time, I couldn't stand the sight of fruits and vegetables. My health was on the ropes, my weight was playing a heavyweight match, and my energy levels barely flickered. But then, the juicing miracle happened.

Juicing was my game-changer. It took me from a junk food aficionado to a full-blown produce enthusiast. It was like a surge of energy, vitality, and life itself coursing through my veins. The weight melted away, my skin turned radiant, and my immune system geared up for battle. Juicing didn't just nourish my body. It also ignited my creativity, made me adventurous, and turned me into a fruit and veggie detective.

In this chapter, you've uncovered the juicing basics: what it is, why it's your health buddy, the how-to's, and the tools of the trade. You've soaked in some tips and tricks to supercharge your juicing adventure—making it smoother, quicker, more fun, and extra nourishing. You've unlocked the secret to picking the juicer that suits you best, the art of prepping fruits and veggies, storing and sipping your liquid gold, and conquering the clean-up mission.

But hold tight because your juicing journey is just getting started. In the next chapter, brace yourself for a juicy encounter with your fruity and veggie co-stars. We're talking nutrition, health perks, flavor fireworks, dream duos, and a treasure trove of fruit and veggie wisdom.

You're about to enter a world of juicy wonders from selection to prep, chopping to juicing!

2

MEET YOUR FRUITS AND VEGGIES

Organic enthusiasts hail organic produce as the king of the grocery jungle, boasting health benefits and eco-friendliness. Imagine kale striking a pose and yelling, "I'm organic, hear me crunch!" On the flip side, skeptics, the doubting tomatoes, argue it's pricier than a gourmet latte and harder to find than your car keys on a Monday morning.

Going organic means steering clear of synthetic pesticides, fertilizers, hormones, and antibiotics, potentially resulting in lower exposure to pesky chemicals. Plus, it's a win for the environment, with less soil erosion, cleaner water, and a lighter carbon footprint. But here's the kicker —going organic demands more land, manpower, and resources, making it a bit of a splurge and a tad out of reach for many (Emily, 2022).

When it comes to nutrition, studies say the differences between organic and regular produce are like splitting hairs, and some veggies, like avocados and broccoli, might not need that organic badge. On the flip side, strawberries, spinach, grapes, apples, tomatoes, and celery pack a punch of pesticides, making the organic choice more tempting.

For those stretching every dollar, frozen veggies are a lifesaver. They're the budget-friendly treasures of the freezer aisle, offering quality without breaking the bank. Now, the question is: Organic or conventional? It's all up to personal preference. If organic options seem out of reach or just too pricey, remember that once adequately washed, traditional veggies remain a solid nutrition choice.

No matter the label, the golden rule stands strong—load up on fruits and veggies daily. They're the real lead characters in your nutrition story, whether they wear the organic label or not.

ORGANIC OR CONVENTIONAL

Embarking on the juicing journey? Buckle up; we're about to unveil the intricacies of this fruity and veggie spectacle, with conventional fruits and veggies taking center stage in your juicing escapade. Sounds safe, right? But hold on for the twist—the plot thickens with a sprinkle of pesticides and some not-so-friendly chemicals on this seemingly innocent produce. Juicing, our protagonist, manages to kick some of these intruders out, but alas, not all make a grand exit.

Enter the lead of the produce aisle—the organic protagonist. Grown without the villainous synthetic pesticides, fertilizers, or GMOs, these goodies bring a bonus round: Studies have shown they pack a serious punch with higher vitamin and mineral levels (Emily, 2022). And they're not just the MVPs of nutrition. They double as environmental saints, combating soil erosion, water pollution, and greenhouse gas emissions.

Pump those brakes, my friends! Organic produce, despite its cape, doesn't come without its own set of challenges. This is the VIP section—fancy, but it hits the wallet a bit harder. Shorter shelf life? Oh, absolutely! Pests' playground? You betcha! And, oh, it might play a game of hide-and-seek, depending on the season and location. So, here's where the juicer stands at the crossroads, with the age-old dilemma: conventional or organic?

But wait, don't lock yourself into just one storyline. Juicing can be a choose-your-own-adventure tale! Mix it up! Go organic for the high-risk produce—those apples, celery, spinach, and strawberries that might have partied too hard with pesticides (Good Food, 2019). Let the laid-back crew—avocados, bananas, cabbage, and onions—rock the conventional vibe.

- **Pro tip:** Before the juicing curtain rises, give your produce a good scrub. Bid farewell to dirt, wave off bacteria, and let lingering chemicals make their grand exit.

In this juicy narrative, the power is in your hands. You get to choose between conventional and organic, or perhaps you want a little bit of both. So, here's a cheers to a blended and balanced adventure! May your juicer whir with excitement and your taste buds dance in delight. Juicing, after all, is not just a journey; it's a flavorful odyssey.

ORGANIC VS. NATURAL

Organic food is not merely a label. It's a way of life and a commitment to a standard set by the U.S. Department of Agriculture (USDA) (Revis, 2019). This organic VIP club is exclusive, demanding that its members, the fruits and vegetables, be grown and processed without the companionship of synthetic pesticides, fertilizers, GMOs, irradiation, antibiotics, or growth hormones. It's the USDA's firm way of saying, "No artificial stuff, please!" Yet, in the realm of wholesome eating, organic and natural aren't exactly bosom buddies.

Visualize natural as the cool cousin. The term implies an absence of artificial ingredients or preservatives, but it doesn't guarantee a seamless entry into the organic goodness club. Natural foods, in their carefree dance, might still tango with conventional methods, greeting pesticides and fertilizers with a nonchalant shrug. And here's where the narrative takes a twist: Natural food doesn't require the USDA's nod of approval. Instead, it's a free-spirit labeling optional.

Alright, let's dive into the great debate: Does organic wear the superhero cape in the grocery cityscape? The journey for answers is as riveting as a page from a Dan Brown thriller. Some research champions organic produce for its reduced pesticide residues, fewer antibiotic-resistant bugs, and lesser heavy metal burdens. Yet, there's another camp that touts organic's superior nutrient profile—boasting richer vitamins, minerals, antioxidants, and phytochemicals.

Here's the kicker: These differences might not be as black and white as they initially seem. It's like a party where soil quality, climate, crop variety, storage time, and cooking methods RSVP. The nuances of these factors blur the lines of the organic tale, turning it into a complex dance where the label isn't the sole star, but the supporting cast matters too (Revis, 2019).

So, while the label does carry weight, it's how you treat your food that steals the spotlight. Adopt the culinary finesse of Gordon Ramsay—wash, peel, and juice with master chef precision. Your kitchen transforms into the stage for the real magic, where, whether it's organic or not, the alchemy happens. The love and attention you infuse into your culinary creations become the secret ingredients of a vibrant and wholesome life.

This narrative isn't just about choosing organic for the sake of a label. It's about embracing a lifestyle that values the journey of food from farm to table. It's a celebration of conscious choices and mindful consumption. So, wield that peeler and juicer with intent, for in the heart of your kitchen, amidst the chopping and blending, lies the true alchemy—a flavorful journey towards a healthier, more delightful life.

The real magic isn't in the label. Instead, it's in the culinary adventures you embark upon in your very own kitchen. Cheers to the fruity masters—the mindful chefs crafting wellness, one organic or natural bite at a time!

HOW TO BALANCE ORGANIC AND CONVENTIONAL

Embarking on a journey toward a healthier and more organic lifestyle, I was initially deterred by the perceived costliness of organic produce. The shiny allure of the organic section in the supermarket seemed financially elusive, and I often found myself settling for conventional options with a silent hope that they weren't laden with harmful chemicals.

However, my outlook transformed when I uncovered a treasure trove of tips and hacks that made navigating the organic food landscape on a budget not only possible but surprisingly empowering. The concept of selective organic shopping became a guiding principle because I could choose which products were most deserving of my organic investment.

Understanding the Environmental Working Group's "Clean 15" and "Dirty Dozen" lists turned into a revelation (Emily, 2022). These lists offered a roadmap for discerning where conventional options sufficed and where it was worth splurging on the organic variant.

Avocados and pineapples, being low in pesticide residues, earned their place on the "Clean 15" greenlight list. Alternatively, strawberries, spinach, and apples found themselves on the "Dirty Dozen" cautionary roster (Emily, 2022).

My exploration expanded to local farmers' markets and community-supported agriculture (CSA) programs, proving to be not only a source of fresh and organic produce but also a budget-friendly alternative to traditional supermarkets. Supporting local farmers while reducing my carbon footprint became a win-win scenario.

Buying in bulk or in-season became a strategic maneuver, unlocking lower prices and a wider variety of options. Coupon clipping, sales scouting, and loyalty programs evolved into my budgetary secret weapons. Finding online discounts, seeking supermarket deals, or leveraging loyalty rewards became my organic currency.

Planning meals ahead and cooking at home emerged as budget-saving practices. Armed with meticulous lists, I sidestepped impulse purchases and food waste, opting for thoughtful meal planning and clever usage of leftovers to maximize my organic bounty. For the adventurous at heart, delving into growing my own food or joining a community garden added an extra layer of satisfaction.

Suddenly, my windowsill or backyard became a canvas for cultivating an organic haven. Flexibility and creativity became trusted companions as I experimented with new recipes or substituted conventional ingredients with organic alternatives. In essence, these discovered tips and hacks not only facilitated a delicate equilibrium between health-conscious choices and budget constraints but also transformed my once-regretful stroll past the organic aisle into a strategic, satisfying, and empowering organic adventure.

May these insights guide you on your personalized journey toward organic bliss, proving that a commitment to health need not break the bank!

UNDERSTANDING YOUR FRUITS AND VEGETABLES

Ladies and gentlemen, welcome to the grand stage of juicing, where fruits and veggies take the spotlight in a health-packed extravaganza! We're not just talking about your regular produce; we're talking about the luminaries of the juicing universe. Get ready for a taste sensation and a nutrient-packed El Toro ride!

Papaya: The Digestive Dynamo!

Papaya is more than just a tropical delight. It's your digestive dynamo. Thanks to papain—an enzyme with the magical ability to break down proteins—papaya is your go-to remedy for easing digestion issues (Simkins, n.d). While it might not be the juicer's best friend, it certainly knows how to dazzle in blender drinks and smoothies. To prepare papaya for its juicy debut, gracefully peel it and remove the seeds—the key to smooth blending. Let the papaya party begin!

- **Safety tip:** When handling papaya, ensure your peeling skills are top-notch to avoid any accidental finger foxtrots.

Beets: Hydration Maestros!

Beets, the hydration maestros, bring a symphony of electrolytes like sodium and potassium to the juicing stage

(TeamReboot, 2022). Their vibrant color is not just for show; it's a sign of the rich betalains, powerful antioxidants that fend off oxidative stress and inflammation. These crimson wonders are not just a treat for the eyes but also a boost for the immune system, blood pressure, and digestion. They're a bit finicky to peel, but that's a small price to pay for their benefits. Give them a thorough wash a gentle peel, and let the beet juicing symphony commence!

- **Safety tip:** Beets have a knack for staining, so wear your kitchen cape and prepare for the vibrant aftermath.

Berries: The Antioxidant Avengers!

Berries, the antioxidant Captain Americas, don't just bring color and flavor; they're here to wage war against cellular damage. These little powerhouses are antiviral, antibacterial, and downright good for the blood (Simkins, n.d). From blueberries battling urinary infections to strawberries swooping in for cardiovascular health, each berry has its unique superpower. While they might be a bit of a workout for the juicer, their health benefits make every blend worth it. Give them a good wash, strip away any stems or leaves, and let the berry juicing spectacle begin!

- **Safety tip:** Berry stems might be tiny, but they can be real troublemakers. Evict them before the juicing showdown.

Cucumbers: Cool as a Cucumber Ninjas!

Cucumbers, the cool ninjas of hydration, don't just bring freshness. They also come packed with vitamin K, phosphorus, and silica, supporting bone health, skin radiance, and kidney function (TeamReboot, 2022). Mostly water, they form a perfect base for your juices. Whether you decide to keep their skin on for an extra nutrient punch or opt for the organic commando, cucumbers are your go-to for flushing out toxins, reducing swelling, and hydrating the body. Give them a good wash, a trim at the ends, and let the cucumber juicing Zen unfold!

- **Safety tip:** Watch out for the slippery cucumber moves. Keep those fingers safe during preparation.

Pineapples: Anti-Inflammatory Pineapple Partiers!

Pineapples, the anti-inflammatory party planners, are not just here to add a tropical flair to your juice. They dissolve blood clots thanks to bromelain, a digestive enzyme that also knows how to break down proteins (Simkins, n.d). Peeling them might seem like preparing for a tropical getaway, but once you get past the tough exterior, it's a pineapple party in the juicer. Cut them into chunks, bid farewell to the core, and let the pineapple juicing festivities begin!

- **Safety tip:** Pineapples might look sweet, but be careful with those skins. These golden globes, adorned with a crown of spiky leaves, harbor a concealed danger within their rugged skins.

Tomatoes: Lycopene Legends!

Tomatoes, the lycopene legends, are not just a salad staple. They're also your ticket to a lower risk of cancer and a heart-healthy lifestyle (Simkins, n.d). These red wonders blend well with veggies, and their taste is a treat for your taste buds. Wash them well, cut them into quarters, and let the tomato juicing saga unfold. But remember, raw tomatoes are a different breed than their cooked cousins; don't expect tomato sauce to have the same invigorating effect as tomato juice.

- **Safety tip:** A sharp knife is your sidekick when slicing through these juicy legends.

Peaches: Juicy Immunity Juggernauts!

Peaches, the juicy immunity juggernauts, aren't just a summer delight. They're packed with vitamins C and A, calcium, and potassium (TeamReboot, 2022). From boosting the immune system to protecting eyesight, strengthening bones, and supporting the heart, peaches are your go-to for tasty and nutritious juice. Give them a good wash, bid the pits farewell, and let the peach juicing revelry begin!

- **Safety tip:** The pit might be the peach's secret weapon, but it's not juicer or blender-friendly. Remove it with care.

Grapes: Anti-Aging Grape Glam Squad!

Grapes, the anti-aging glam squad, bring resveratrol, quercetin, and anthocyanins to the juice party. Whether you juice them whole or halved, these tiny delights have anti-inflammatory, anti-cancer, and anti-aging properties (TeamReboot, 2022). Wash them well, destem, and let the grape juicing glamour commence!

- **Safety tip:** Ensure no stray stems are photobombing your grape juice—they might not be as sweet as the grapes.

Apples: Versatile Antioxidant VIPs!

Apples, the versatile antioxidant VIPs, are more than just a teacher's gift. They cleanse your digestive palace, boost immunity, and complement almost any fruit or veg (Simkins, n.d). Wash them well, say goodbye to the stems and seeds, and let the apple juicing adventure begin!

- **Safety tip:** An apple a day keeps the doctor away, but a safe cut keeps accidents at bay. Watch those fingers!

Juice isn't just a beverage; it's a front-row seat to a fruit and veggie spectacle. So, fasten your seatbelts, cue the juicer, and let the juicing circus take you on an unforgettable ride!

WHAT TO DO WITH THE PULP

I have a secret, and it's time to spill the (green) beans: I am a juice addict. Ever since my first encounter with a gleaming juicer, I've been entranced by the allure of freshly extracted liquid goodness. The symphony of flavors, the vibrant colors, and the promise of a healthier me—it was irresistible.

However, there's a catch, a pulpable dilemma, to be precise. It's the aftermath, the wet and mushy pulp of my liquid escapades. It seemed criminal to toss away what felt like a graveyard of nutrients and fiber, a wasteful goodbye to all the good stuff.

So, I embarked on a quest—an adventure searching for the holy grail of "what to do with juice pulp." Lo and behold, a world of possibilities unveiled itself. Muffins, crackers, burgers, soups, salads, and even dog treats. The options were as diverse as the fruits and veggies I'd been juicing.

My excitement reached a culinary crescendo. I was the maestro of juice pulp, conducting a symphony of flavors with my secret ingredient. Each day was a new recipe, a new experiment, and I felt like a culinary genius—turning what was once waste into gastronomic wonders. Here are some creative and eco-friendly ways to re-use and recycle your pulp (Frey, 2020):

Garden Fertilizer

In your garden, leafy greens and root vegetables emerge as the true champions. Compost the pulp and use it as a natural fertilizer for your plants. Combine it with other organic materials like leaves, grass clippings, coffee grounds, or eggshells in your compost bin or pile.

Your leftover pulp, rich in a diverse array of nutrients, becomes the secret weapon in your quest for garden glory. As the pulp breaks down, it releases valuable elements into the soil, providing nourishment that your plants will gladly lap up. This process not only enriches the soil with organic matter but also helps retain moisture and ward off weeds.

Dog Treats

Even your furry friend can partake in the joy of juice pulp. Create healthy and delicious dog treats by combining dog-safe juice pulp with oats, peanut butter, and eggs. Roll the mixture into small balls, bake until golden brown, and let them cool before presenting your dog with a homemade delight. Carrot pulp, with its subtle sweetness, is particularly well-received in the canine world.

Spreads

Take your taste buds on an Indiana Jones adventure with spreads crafted from juice pulp. Hummus, pesto, and cream cheese are just a blender away. Combine the pulp with nuts, seeds, herbs, spices, olive oil, or yogurt, and blend until the mixture achieves a smooth and creamy consistency.

Almond pulp and leafy greens shine in this category. Create a vegan basil pesto where almond pulp (from making almond milk) meets basil leaves, garlic cloves, lemon juice, nutritional yeast (optional), salt, pepper, and olive oil. It's a spreadable symphony of flavors that adds a nutritious punch to your sandwiches, salads, wraps, or dips.

Popsicles

Embrace the summertime harder than Will Smith by turning juice pulp into refreshing popsicles. Blend the pulp with water or milk, add sugar if desired, pour into popsicle molds, freeze, and enjoy your own, healthy popsicles. Fruit pulp, being naturally sweet, is an ideal candidate for this frozen treat. Freeze the remnants of your juicing adventure in ice cube trays, and they become convenient frozen boosters for your next smoothie.

Breakfast

Sprinkle a dash of health onto your morning routine by topping oatmeal, yogurt, or cereal with juice pulp. Stir it in before serving for an extra burst of flavor and texture. Enhance the experience with nuts, seeds, dried fruits, or honey for added crunch and sweetness. Fruit pulp, with its vibrant and sweet profile, is a natural fit. Top your oatmeal with pulp from apples and a hint of cinnamon for a breakfast that's as nutritious as it is delicious.

Fruit Leather

By spreading juice pulp on a baking sheet lined with parchment paper and dehydrating it until dry and leathery, you can turn it into a chewy, sweet delicacy. This homemade fruit leather is a healthier alternative to store-bought snacks. Spread the pulp evenly on a baking sheet, drizzle with maple syrup or honey if desired, and dehydrate at a low temperature until the magic happens. Roll up your fruit leather, and you've got a portable, fruity snack. Berries and apples take center stage in this endeavor.

Smoothies

Elevate your smoothie game by incorporating juice pulp. Whether it's the remnants of a fruit fiesta or a green dream, pulp adds an extra layer of fiber and nutrients to your favorite blend. Simply toss the pulp into the blender with your other smoothie ingredients, blend until smooth, and enjoy the thick and satisfying result. Berries, in particular, work wonders in this domain. Create a berry smoothie where pulp from various berries meets yogurt, milk, honey, and ice—a refreshing and nutrient-packed delight.

Raw Pulp Crackers

Is your carrot pulp feeling left out after its juicing adventure? Fear not! We're about to turn it into something crunchy and delightful: vegan and gluten-free pulp crackers. For an added kick, combine your carrot (or other veggie) pulp with flax seeds, a dash of water, a hint of salt and pepper, and your favorite herbs or spices. Dehydrate them in the oven or a dehydrator until they're crisp and ready to rock. These crackers are versatile companions, pairing perfectly with hummus, guacamole, cheese, or any dip that gets your taste buds dancing.

Baked Goods

Baking meets juicing, like Batman and Robin, in a delightful fusion of flavors and nutrition. Juice pulp, whether it's a medley of leafy greens or vibrant root vegetables, becomes a star ingredient in muffins, breads, cookies, and cakes. The pulp not only introduces moisture and sweetness but also sneaks in an array of nutrients. It's a game-changer that allows you to reduce the reliance on oil or butter in your baking endeavors.

Consider spinach and banana muffins, where the pulp from these ingredients takes a basic muffin recipe to a whole new level. For those on the go, you can create your own healthy baking mixes by combining juice pulp with flour, baking powder, and salt. When the baking mood strikes, simply add your preferred wet ingredients like eggs, milk, and oil. It's a win-win for your taste buds and your health.

Vegan Basil Pesto

Ever wondered what to do with that almond pulp after squeezing out almond milk? Well, put on your culinary cap because here's a fantastic solution: Vegan basil pesto. Gather up almond pulp, fresh basil leaves, a hint of garlic, a splash of lemon juice, nutritional yeast for that cheesy kick, and the classic duo of salt and pepper. Drizzle in some olive oil, blend it all into a glorious green concoction, and voilà! You've got a vegan basil pesto ready to steal the show. Use it as a spread for your morning toast, a dip for your veggie sticks, or the secret sauce for your pasta and salads. This pesto isn't just a sauce; it's a flavor symphony.

Soup Broth

Transform your juice pulp like Optimus Prime into a rich and nutritious soup broth that forms the foundation for soups, stews, curries, or risottos. This versatile broth requires nothing more than water or broth, salt, pepper, spices, and an abundance of vegetable pulp. Fresh or frozen, the pulp works its magic.

Boil the concoction, add your seasonings, let it simmer for about an hour, and voila! You have a hearty broth ready to elevate your culinary creations. Carrot and ginger soup broth, for instance, blends the pulp from these ingredients with water or broth, salt, and pepper, delivering a flavorful base for your next kitchen masterpiece.

These recipes are more than just culinary creations; they're a culinary revolution, turning what was once waste into wonders for your palate. Get ready to elevate your kitchen game to LeBron standards with these simple yet genius ways to transform pulp into edible delights!

KEY TAKEAWAYS

Welcome to the juicing jungle, where the choice between organic and conventional produce feels like a riddle wrapped in a mystery inside a kale leaf. This chapter served as your trusty guide, weaving through the vine of opinions and the orchard of information to help you emerge unscathed and with the perfect ingredients for your liquid concoctions.

Here are the key takeaways from this chapter:

- First things first, let's talk safety—nobody wants a side of pesticides with their morning smoothie.

We delved into whether it was safe to invite conventional fruits and veggies to the juicing party, shedding light on potential pesticide gatecrashers. Then, we blended in the pros and cons of both organic and conventional produce, giving you the lowdown on what is accessible, what doesn't break the bank, and what packs a nutritional punch.

- Next, we ventured into the mysterious realm of organic. What does it really mean? We unraveled the organic code, courtesy of the USDA, highlighting the stringent standards that separated the organic apples from the non-organic oranges. And just so you know, organic and natural? Not the same. We were talking apples and oranges, people. We also threw a spotlight on the burning question: Is organic food safer or just fancier? It is like a suspense thriller with fewer car chases but more nutrient drama.
- Now, let's break down the cast of characters in your juicing escapade—the fruits and veggies. Each one got its own moment in the spotlight, revealing its nutritional prowess and how it could turn your body into a powerhouse. Safety tips for each were dished out like backstage passes, ensuring your juicing experience was a star-studded (and safe!) affair.
- You were introduced to the ultimate pulp fiction (eat your heart out, Mr. Tarantino). What was

once trash is now a treasure trove of culinary potential. Practical tips and suggestions flow like a smoothie fountain in this chapter, offering you creative alternatives to ditching the pulp. It's a kitchen revolution, one peel at a time.

I hope you're feeling like a juicing produce connoisseur. Because when it comes to juicing, knowledge is juice power.

This chapter was your ticket to juicing enlightenment—packed with wisdom, a smidge of humor, and enough tips to make your kitchen the stage for a produce-powered drama—as a teaser for the next chapter: "Making It Work."

3

MAKING IT WORK

Who has the time to become a produce-chopping, juice-spilling, kitchen-cleaning wizard when you have a million things to do? Work, family, hobbies, Netflix... Not me, no thank you! I barely had time to eat, let alone juice.

I thought juicing meant I had to squeeze every drop of liquid from a bunch of fruits and veggies and then scrub the sticky mess. But then, in a miraculous turn of events, I stumbled upon the secrets of juicing for the time-crunched. It was like discovering the Holy Grail of convenience in the world of nutrition.

For instance, I always clean my juicer immediately after use. Only once it's spotless do I indulge in the juice. It serves as a reward for my effort. Trust me, you don't want to deal with moldy pulp and fermented juice. And let's talk about my juicer—the wider the chute, the better it is for juicing. That means I don't have to slice and dice my fruits and veggies into tiny, absurdly precise pieces. It's like my juicer is saying, "Bring on the whole carrots, cucumbers, and apples, my friend!"

Now, I can enjoy fresh and delicious juice every morning without wasting my precious time. Juicing has become part of my lifestyle, and I feel more alive, alert, and awesome than ever before. And you can too! In this chapter, I'm spilling (but not literally) all my secrets to make juicing simple, fun, and satisfying for busy people like you.

JUICING TIPS AND HACKS: PLANNING

Do you remember what we covered in the previous chapter about buying your produce in bulk, in local stores, and in season? This advice is not only good for your wallet and the environment but also for your juicing routine. By preparing your produce and storing it properly for juicing in advance, you can make things much easier for yourself and save a heck of a lot of time.

I simply love juicing and know how important it is to have fresh and tasty produce ready to go. But sometimes, life gets in the way, and I don't have time to wash, chop, and store my fruits and vegetables daily. That's why preparing and storing the produce properly for juicing in advance can make a huge difference in your juicing experience. Why waste your precious time and energy on chopping, slicing, and dicing your fruits and veggies when you can just toss them in a blender and call it a day? Not only will you save yourself from the hassle of knife skills, but you will also preserve the freshness and nutrition of your produce and prevent it from rotting and turning into compost.

For example, batch juicing is a time-saving method where you prepare and juice a variety of fruits and veggies at once. Wash, chop, and let your juicer transform the colorful mix into a refreshing concoction. Store the freshly squeezed juice in airtight containers in the fridge for convenient sipping throughout the week.

Starting with one juice a day is a step forward. Over time, you might feel encouraged to try a full 'cleanse'. The following tips from *Jade's Juicy Bar* to your kitchen will prove essential for anyone planning a single-day, three-day, or seven-day cleanse:

- **Consider your goals:** Before beginning your juice cleanse, take a step back and ask yourself: What am I hoping to achieve with this cleanse? Am I trying to lose weight? Boost my energy? Ease any inflammation or pain? Setting clear health objectives will give you the motivation you need to conquer this cleanse and give you a glow that can outshine a supernova.
- **Stay motivated:** Don't be disheartened if the first day comes to an end and you're not feeling your

best. The most challenging part is often the initial day, even for those who've done it before. Continue throughout the entire cleanse period, and monitor your progress.

- **Keep a journal:** Before embarking on your cleanse journey, get a notebook or journal to keep track of your emotions. Evaluate its effectiveness later by recording how you felt in the days leading up to the cleanse. Improvements in your skin, constant hunger, or satisfaction from certain juices and smoothies can be identified. Determine which flavors were a homerun and which ones were a swing and a miss (Kogler, 2016).
- **Plan your recipes:** Planning your juice recipes will help you research and be better equipped in the kitchen during your cleanse.
- **Early preparation:** To get a head start, opt for lighter meals a couple of days before commencing your cleanse. In other words, avoid indulging in a buffet feast the night before. Be mindful of potential withdrawal symptoms if you're a caffeine enthusiast. Minimize these effects by gradually reducing your coffee and tea intake in the days leading up to your cleanse.
- **Be prepared for cravings:** It's perfectly normal for thoughts of food to surface unexpectedly. Your body is adjusting to a cleanse since it's accustomed to a routine that involves regular meals. Take a sip

of juice whenever a craving strikes, then continue your day. You can handle it!

- **Choose a cleanse that's right for you:** Taking on a three-, seven-, or ten-day cleanse straight off the bat might prove challenging, potentially discouraging you from juicing altogether. Work your way up to longer durations by beginning with a maximum three-day cleanse. Even a single-day cleanse can yield amazing results. Every step in the right direction counts. Consider your wellness and dietary concerns when choosing a cleanse (Clarke, 2019).
- **Choose fruit and vegetables wisely:** If you're planning to go on a juice fast, you better be picky about your fruits and veggies. Don't settle for the cheap stuff that's sprayed with chemicals and loaded with metals. Go for the organic ones that have more antioxidants and less junk. Trust me, you don't want to be drinking pesticide juice for days. It's bad enough that you're giving up solid food—at least make sure your liquid diet is clean and healthy. For more cost-effective alternatives, you could try big box stores.
- **Address the protein factor:** Muscles need protein for strength and satisfaction. Fruits and veggies lack protein, so include high-protein veggies in your cleanse to prevent muscle loss, a growling stomach, and violent mood swings. Otherwise, you'll end up looking like a skeleton and feeling

low on energy. For instance, consider the protein content in an 8 oz (227 g) serving of these raw veggies (How to juice, 2023):

- kale (0.25 oz or 7 g of protein)
- watercress (0.18 oz or 5 g of protein)
- broccoli (0.18 oz or 5 g of protein)
- baby spinach (0.18 oz or 5 g of protein)
- cabbage (0.11 oz or 3 g protein)

Now that you have a clear idea of how to plan your juicing efficiently, it's time to dive into the next step: preparation. Preparing your ingredients for juicing is essential not only for the quality and taste of your juice but also for your health and safety. Juicing is an art, and your ingredients are your paintbrush and canvas. Handle them skillfully, and you will create a masterpiece of flavor and wellness.

PREPARATION

To peel or not to peel, is indeed the dilemma we face in the juicy kingdom of fruits and veggies. Some produce, like apples, pears, and the ever-so-lovable carrots, boast peels packed with more nutrients than an Olympian's breakfast. On the flip side, there are those with peels so tough and bitter that they're like the uninvited guests at a party—looking at you, oranges, grapefruits, pineapples, and beets. Rule of thumb: Peel anything you wouldn't munch on like a hungry rabbit.

Now, let's dive into the seed saga. Some seeds, like watermelon, pomegranate, and lemon, add a delightful crunch to your juice party. Others, such as apricot and cherry seeds, are like the party poopers of the seed world. The rule here? Kick out the big and the hard seeds. Nobody needs that kind of drama in their juice life.

And lo, we reach the grand finale: To remove or not to remove. Can you juice stems, leaves, and cores? Or should you kick them to the curb like last year's fashion? It's like fruit and veggie survival of the fittest. Some are juice-worthy, while others are destined for a different calling, like becoming compost champions.

These questions are an odyssey into the vibrant lifestyle of juicing, where each glass is a celebration of flavors and a cascade of nutrients. The following is a comprehensive guide, where I'll unravel the secrets of juicing, focusing on a kaleidoscope of fruits and unveiling tips and techniques to elevate your juicing experience (Sexner, 2015):

- **Apples:** Indulge in a perfect balance of sweetness and tartness as you sink into the world of apple-infused potions. Keep those apples whole and unpeeled; the peels are where the magic lies. The skin, a treasure trove of nutrients, adds depth to

your juice. Choose varieties like Granny Smith for a tangy kick or Gala for a sweeter melody.
- **Pineapples:** Let your taste buds dance with the tropical rhythm of pineapples. A quartet of quarters with the skin removed ensures a burst of flavor. Pineapple cores, a fiber-rich bonus, contribute to a textured masterpiece. Juice with citrus fruits for a zesty symphony.
- **Oranges and grapefruits:** Citrusy delights, oranges and grapefruits bring a burst of sunshine to your juices. Peel them gracefully before juicing to avoid the bitter undertones of the peel. Grinding and pressing elevate these fruits to their juiciest potential. Experiment with blends for a citrus extravaganza.
- **Lemons and limes:** Add a zing to your concoctions with the citrusy allure of lemons and limes. For the brave, grind with the peel on for an extra kick. Alternatively, peel for a smoother experience. The aromatic oils in the peel elevate your juice to a sensory masterpiece.
- **Mangos and papayas:** Unleash the tropics into your juicing realm with mangos and papayas. Blend these exotic wonders before introducing them to your juice for a creamy texture. Marry them with citrus fruits for a harmonious tropical symphony.
- **Melons:** Indulge in the sweetness of melons—watermelon, honeydew, and cantaloupe—for a

hydrating and refreshing base. Peel watermelon for optimal sweetness and de-seed others to avoid bitterness. Experiment with berry and mint infusions for a summery delight.
- **Leafy vegetables:** Enter the green haven of kale, spinach, and Swiss chard, nutritional powerhouses that bring a verdant touch to your juices. Keep those stems—they pack a flavor punch. Merge with apples or citrus fruits for a balanced bouquet of taste.
- **Berries:** Berries, tiny explosions of color and antioxidants, demand a special approach. Transform them into a puree before juicing them with other fruits. Add berry puree to various blends for a visual and flavorful treat.
- **Beets:** Earthiness meets sweetness with beets, providing a vibrant hue to your juices. Clean them thoroughly, removing the top and, if small, the bottom skinny part. Beets pair splendidly with carrots and apples for a nutrient-rich experience.
- **Passion fruit:** Elevate your juice with the tangy and exotic notes of passion fruit. Scoop out those seeds and infuse them into your elixir for a delightful crunch. A touch of passion fruit adds an unexpected twist.
- **Carrots:** Carrots, the unsung heroes of juicing, bring natural sweetness and a burst of color. Top ends off, they blend harmoniously with citrus fruits and ginger for a refreshing kick.

- **Cucumbers:** Infuse your juice with the crisp and hydrating essence of cucumbers. Cleanse them with an antimicrobial wash, peel for light-colored juices, or leave the skin on for a robust flavor. Please remember to peel if there is wax on the cucumber. These juicy wonders mingle beautifully with mint and citrus fruits for a revitalizing experience.

Raise your glass to the symphony of flavors and nutrients that juicing unveils. This guide, your key to juicing mastery, has unraveled the secrets of fruits, tips, and techniques. From deciding whether to peel or not to peel, dealing with seeds, to the meticulous preparation of specific fruits, you're now equipped to create juices that are not just healthful but a celebration of taste. Cheers to your vibrant and flavorful journey into the world of juicing.

CORRECTLY STORING JUICE

Juicing—the art of turning veggies into Hulk-green goodness and transforming fruits into liquid rainbows. Freshly squeezed juice is like the elixir of life or the nectar of the gods. Ideally, you'd gulp it down on the spot. But alas, reality slaps us with work, travel, and life's grand spectacles, making the immediate juice chug-a-thon a rare feat.

So, what's a juice lover to do? Behold, the sacred act of juice storage! Your vibrant concoction should be sealed in an airtight glass container, ready to defy time and space. If you're using a cold-presser juicer, you could store your juice longer.

To battle the evil forces of nutrient degradation, it's wise to arm yourself with airtight glass containers. The closer you fill them to the brim, the better. It's like giving your juice a fortress against the villainous oxygen, the archnemesis of all things fresh and nutritious.

Now, for an antioxidant-packed refresher, toss in a citrus wedge—your juice's trusty sidekick, if you will. Lemon, lime, or grapefruit will do the trick. They boost Vitamin C and citric acid, plus squeezing lemon over avocados will thwart browning. This part is where batch juicing saves the day.

Be cautious, juice enthusiast. Your concoction has a lifespan of 24-48 hours in the fridge—maybe a bit more if you're pushing it to 72 hours (*Tips for storing juice,* n.d.). Beyond that, freeze it, but thaw it in the fridge, not at room temperature. Remember, liquids expand when frozen, so leave some room in the container to avoid a frosty mess in the freezer.

And why do apples turn into brown, sob stories so quickly? Blame it on oxidation that happens when nutrients meet their oxygen adversary.

So, juice on, oh juice alchemist, and may your preparations stay fresher than a morning breeze in a citrus grove!

STORING FRUITS AND VEGGIES

Ah, the art of preserving the kingdom of fruits and veggies, where each lord and lady demands their own royal treatment. Here's a scroll of wisdom on how to keep your produce realm in pristine condition (Frey, 2021):

- **Apples:** Treat them with the respect they deserve. At room temperature, they'll be your loyal subjects for about a week. In the chilly confines of the royal refrigerator, their loyalty extends to a month or two. For an extra layer of protection, seal them in a plastic ziplock bag. And before pressing them into juice duty, let them chill in the refrigerator for a few hours.
- **Cucumbers:** These delicate courtiers prefer room temperature but demand solitude. Keep them away from other fruits and vegetables, for they are easily influenced by the natural gas (ethylene) emitted by other vegetables. Beware, if stored below 50 degrees, they might turn traitor, becoming slimy and developing soft spots. Even so, a brief sojourn in the refrigerator before juicing is recommended.
- **Beets:** Remove their crowns and scrub their bottoms thoroughly. If they are petite in size, bid

farewell to the skinny bottom part. Place them in a perforated plastic bag and stash them in the coldest nook of your refrigerator—typically the bottom shelf or the crisper drawer. Stored this way, beets will pledge allegiance to your juicing cause for up to three months.
- **Berries:** These tiny, fleshy jesters might not be bursting with liquid, but they're full of potential. A blender becomes their ally, transforming them into a puree fit for royal juice. For color and flavor infusion, a gentle process and press with other ingredients in your recipe is recommended.
- **Carrots:** The noble carrots, valiant yet dirty, bid farewell to their tops. Before they enter the juicing battlefield, let them chill in the refrigerator for a few hours.
- **Celery:** Keep this green lord fresh by giving it a royal bath, cutting it, and submerging it in filtered water in an airtight container. If untouched, strip away its plastic regalia and store it whole, either uncovered in the refrigerator or swathed in tinfoil (to let ethylene escape and prevent hastened spoilage).
- **Leafy vegetables:** Here, the stems are the superstars. Do not strip them of their glory— they're laden with flavor and juice. Before they embark on the juicing quest, let them chill in the refrigerator.

Preparing fruits and vegetables for juicing might seem like a daunting task, especially if it's part of your daily routine. However, with the right knowledge and techniques, juicing can easily become an integral and hassle-free part of your day.

By prepping and storing your produce ahead of time, you streamline the juicing process, making it both time-efficient and enjoyable. Recreate your kitchen as a well-organized space where fresh ingredients are always ready to be transformed into refreshing and nourishing juices. Here's to a well-stocked kitchen and juices that are both delightful and nutritious!

SETTING GOALS

Being a perennial admirer of juicing, I found myself trapped in a cycle of short-lived enthusiasm. I would dive into the world of produce and whip up delightful mixtures, only to abandon them after a fleeting romance. It was not just a culinary dalliance but a financial drain, and worse, I was missing out on the myriad health benefits that juicing could offer.

Then, one day, I decided to flip the script. Armed with determination, I set a concrete goal—juice every single day for a month, meticulously marking my progress on a calendar. But that wasn't enough. I sought companionship in the form of my husband and an online community dedicated to juicers. Here, my husband and I could not only share our recipes but also glean insights, tips, and words of encouragement from fellow enthusiasts.

To my surprise, having a clear goal and a support system transformed my juicing experience. Motivation flowed more abundantly, consistency became second nature, and the positive effects on my energy, skin, and digestion were unmistakable. I ventured into uncharted flavor territories, discovering combinations that I wouldn't have dared to try before.

As the month concluded, I stood tall, having conquered the challenge of juicing every day. A tsunami of pride engulfed me, not just for conquering *Mount Goal*, but for planting the seeds of a habit that I secretly hope will grow into a beanstalk of health and vitality. I mean, move over *Jack and the Beanstalk*. I've got my own version —*Juice and the Kale Stalk*. I'm now waiting for a giant to show up and trade some magic beans for a green smoothie recipe.

Juicing ceased to be a sporadic one-time event; it became a seamless part of my lifestyle, a ritual I relish each day. This journey illuminated a profound truth—setting clear goals and cultivating a support system can be transformative.

To the brave souls embarking on the juicing odyssey, here's a nugget of wisdom: Make your juicer work like it has a Ph.D. in purpose. The transformation is more mind-blowing than turning kale into a green elixir. Juice with intent—because your fruits and veggies have dreams beyond the produce drawer!

Why Do You Need a Goal?

Having a goal in your juicing journey is like giving your juicer a purpose beyond its veggie-juicing duties. It's the North Star that keeps you sipping and juicing with determination. Without it, your juicer might as well take an early retirement.

Now, let's talk goals, those little beacons of motivation that make your juicing venture more exciting than a fruit fiesta.

Consider these possibilities (Leach, 2018):

- **Glowing skin goal:** Drink juice for a natural glow that shines from within.
- **Anti-inflammatory:** Juice can fight against inflammation.
- **Detoxification:** Refresh your body with juice for a natural detox.
- **Weight loss:** Let juice be a helpful companion in your weight loss journey.
- **Improved Digestion:** Support a happy gut with a digestive-friendly juice.
- **Immunity booster:** Juice provides a simple way to boost your immune system.
- **Energy boost:** Consider juice as an alternative for a morning energy lift.

Now, the million-dollar question—how much juice? Well, the conventional juice wisdom suggests sipping on 16-20 ounces a day. But, if you're turning your juice into a meal's understudy, you might need an encore.

And let's not forget the juicing fashion show. Mix it up! Think of your fruits and veggies as runway models, each bringing a unique flair. Spice things up with herbs and spices—your juice's wardrobe deserves an extra pop of flavor and nutrition.

So, set those goals, pour that vibrant brew, and let your juicing journey be a delicious and purposeful adventure!

INTERACTIVE ELEMENT: GOAL SETTING

Here are some guide questions to help you discover your goals in juicing:

1. What improvements do you envision in your mood, relationships, or career as you achieve your health goals, whether it's losing weight, lowering cholesterol, or [insert your reason here]?
2. What will you be able to do that you currently find challenging?
3. How will these changes make your life different?
4. How will the achievement of your health goals influence your overall feelings and well-being?

These questions will help you get clear on the reason you want to juice and help you make juicing part of your new, healthier lifestyle.

TIPS AND STRATEGIES FOR JUICY GOALS:

Here are some strategies to set goals that will make your blender proud (Eatough, 2023):

- **Chop it into sip-sized bits:** Break your juicing goals into smaller, manageable sips. It's like turning a watermelon into bite-sized chunks—easier to savor.
- **Juice gossip:** Spill the juice! Making your goals public adds a splash of accountability. Share your juicing ambitions with friends or family who can cheer you on.
- **SMART Sipping:** Make your goals as SMART as your blender is at crushing veggies:
- **Specific:** Define the exact result you're after (like improving digestion or shedding pounds).
- **Measurable:** Find a way to measure your progress (tracking those bowel movements or pounds lost).
- **Achievable:** Ensure your goal is realistic and fits into your daily grind.
- **Relevant:** Align your juicing goals with your broader health ambitions.
- **Time-bound:** Set a deadline. Give your juicing journey a timeline.

- **Ink it down:** Put your goals on paper. It's like giving your intentions a VIP seat in the front row of your life. Seeing your goals in black and white makes them tangible.
- **Cheers to victories:** Celebrate your successes, including the small wins. Every sip counts! Whether it's a week without digestive hiccups or shedding a few pounds, raise your glass (or juice) to those milestones.

Real-Life Scenarios in Juicing Mastery

Here are some examples to help you understand how to use the aforementioned juicy goal-setting tips:

Scenario 1: Digestive Delight (Improve Digestion Through Juicing)

- **Small sips:** Start with juicing once a day, and then gradually increase the amount.
- **Public pledge:** Share your goal with a supportive friend or family member.
- **SMART digestion:** Specific, measurable (tracking bowel movements), achievable (daily juicing), relevant (to health goals), time-bound (one month).
- **Ink it:** Write down your goal and the juicing routine.
- **Cheers:** Celebrate milestones like a week without digestive issues.

Scenario 2: Weight-Loss Splash (Lose Weight Through Juicing)

- **Small sips:** Begin by replacing one meal with juice before gradually increasing the amount.
- **Public pledge:** Share your weight-loss juicing plan with a supportive friend or family member.
- **SMART loss:** Specific, measurable (tracking weight), achievable (daily juicing), relevant (to health goals), time-bound (three months).
- **Ink it:** Jot down your goal and the steps.
- **Cheers:** Celebrate milestones like losing five pounds.

Now, go forth and juice. Your goals are waiting to be blended into reality!

KEY TAKEAWAYS

Tailor your juicing schedule to align with your goals. It's like having a roadmap for your juicing journey, keeping you motivated and on course.

- **Prepping preparedness:** Prepping your produce in advance is the secret sauce. Extend the shelf life and simplify your juicing process by storing your veggies and fruits smartly.
- **Method to the green madness:** Different veggies need different prep. Roll up those leafy greens

before juicing—a trick to break them down effectively. Learn from the author's experiences to finesse your produce prep game.
- **Chill or freeze:** Know your produce's chill time. Store fruits and veggies accordingly, and don't forget, your juice can join the cool crowd in the fridge or freezer.
- **Prep-ahead efficiency:** Do the groundwork—wash, cut, and store your produce in individual servings. Streamline your juicing routine for maximum efficiency.
- **Goals galore:** Set specific juicing goals to keep the motivation flowing. Whether it's shedding pounds, boosting energy, or nurturing radiant skin—let your goals be your juicing North Star.
- **Start small, dream big:** Begin with achievable goals and gradually level up. It's like juicing 101—master the basics before embarking on the juicing adventures.
- **Recipe roulette:** Don't stick to the same old juicing routine. Mix up your recipes to create a nutrient symphony. It's like giving your taste buds a juicing party—they love variety.
- **Soul-searching questions:** Use the guide questions to uncover your unique juicing goals. Think about the juicing perks that will elevate your life and visualize the juicing triumphs that await you.

- **Strategic goal setting:** Apply the tips and strategies to craft juicing goals that are specific, achievable, and tailor-made for your juicing journey.

This chapter isn't just a guide; it's a treasure trove of juicing mastery. From meticulous planning and savvy preparation to setting goals that align with your juicing aspirations, this chapter helps you unlock the full potential of your juicing experience. Make juicing not just a routine but a delightful and integral part of your healthy lifestyle journey. Juicing, when done right, is not just a sip —it's a lifestyle elixir.

Get ready for a deep dive into rejuvenation with three meticulously crafted juicing detox plans: The dynamic three-day plan, the invigorating five-day plan, and the extended seven-day plan.

These detox plans promise not only a challenge but a rewarding experience, unleashing the multitude of benefits that juicing has to offer. Tailored to align with your juicing goals, these plans are a pathway to a revitalized you.

If you're new to the world of juicing, the three-day plan is your perfect initiation. It offers a sneak peek into the world of juicing detox, allowing you to gauge its suitability for your lifestyle. For those craving an extended adventure and more profound benefits, the seven-day plan awaits.

Both plans are a symphony of nutrient-rich juices meticulously curated to cleanse your body and elevate your energy levels.

Cheers to a healthier, happier you!

4

YOUR SHORT-, MEDIUM-, AND LONG-TERM DETOX PLANS

Over a decade ago, I enthusiastically plunged into the world of juice detox, fueled by the promises of boundless energy and a pristine, toxin-free body, all thanks to an eye-opening documentary. Little did I know, my experience would unfold like a drama, complete with taste twists and unexpected turns!

The initial day was a breeze, sipping on a rainbow of juices—green, red, yellow—all resembling a liquid salad. I convinced myself these elixirs were the secret to vitality. I was a bit hungry, but nothing I couldn't handle.

Then came the second day, a descent into a not-so-pleasant reality. Morning greeted me with a headache, a sore throat, and a bad mood. The first sip of juice tasted like grass infused with dirt. I soldiered on, each bottle bringing a new flavor nightmare—rotten tomatoes with a dash of vinegar, anyone? I almost staged a rebellion with my taste buds.

The third day was a nightmare straight from a horror film. My energy, motivation, and appetite were gone. Juice became my nemesis. I loathed its sight, smell, and sound. Solid, crunchy, salty foods danced in my dreams. "One more day," I muttered through my juice-induced misery.

The fourth day, intended to be the triumphant finale, saw my surrender. A slice of pizza became my liberation, a taste of joy and relief like no other. The remaining juice bottles met a swift demise in the trash, and I vowed never to subject myself to a juice detox again.

Back then, detox symptoms eluded my awareness. Fast forward 15 years, I delved into more research, watched additional documentaries, and broke my sacred vow of never detoxing again. Now, equipped with knowledge, I navigate the detox seas with finesse, turning the negatives into positives like a seasoned sailor taming turbulent waters.

WHAT IS A JUICE CLEANSE?

Alright, my fellow adventurer in the realm of wellness, let's talk about this juice cleanse phenomenon. It's like a short escapade where you ditch the solid stuff and embrace a rainbow of fruit and veggie brews for one to three days.

The master plan? Detox, rejuvenate, and bask in the glory of liquid nutrients. But hold on to your celery sticks—science is still figuring out if it's the real deal. And those lost pounds during the cleanse? Spoiler alert: They might just boomerang back once you reintroduce solid food to the party.

Now, let's uncap the pros and cons of this liquid adventure (MacPherson, 2022):

Pros:

- **Improved health:** It's like a nutrient carnival, with fruits and veggies as the dazzling performers. Your body is in for a vitamin and mineral fiesta!
- **Increased energy:** Some claim to feel completely energized post-juice cleanse. Maybe it's because your digestive system gets a well-deserved break from dealing with solid munchables.
- **Reduced dehydration:** Forget about parched throats; a juice cleanse can be your hydration hero.

Cons:

- **Hunger:** Brace yourself for the symphony of stomach growls as you sip your way through the day. It's like your stomach's encore performance.

- **Weight gain:** That weight you ceremoniously bid farewell to during the cleanse? Well, it's the ultimate boomerang. Surprise!
- **Germ-related infections:** Unpasteurized juice can harbor bacteria, a potential concern for those with chronic conditions, seniors, and kids. If juicing at home, scrub produce well, store in a sealed container, and finish within 24 hours for a safer sip.

So, before you dive into the kaleidoscopic world of liquid rainbows, have a heart-to-heart with your healthcare provider or a nutrition virtuoso. They might just spill the juicy details you need to know!

GETTING READY FOR YOUR DETOX

A "reboot" signals the commencement of a detox adventure, an odyssey where only vegetable and fruit cocktails reign for one to seven glorious days (5-Day, 2013). The concept of a juice cleanse is simple yet profound—purify the body by evicting toxins and simultaneously flood it with revitalizing nourishment. The perks of this reboot extravaganza are nothing short of spectacular (5-Day, 2013):

- **Craving makeover:** Prepare for a taste bud renovation! The juice cleanse acts as an architect, redesigning your palate to crave the wholesome embrace of healthy foods. Fresh juices, crafted from the finest fruits and veggies, become the painters, infusing your body with a masterpiece of essential vitamins B, E and C, minerals (selenium, magnesium, and zinc), and antioxidants, orchestrating an improvement in your overall health.

- **Weight-loss rocket launch:** Want to kickstart your weight-loss journey quickly? Try a juice cleanse—it's like a rocket launch for shedding pounds fast. Although some people resort back to their old eating habits and regain the weight they lost, many have been able to keep off the weight by eating healthier after the cleanse. It's almost like your palate is "rebooted" and doesn't crave the old food.
- **Immune system bodyguard:** Envision your immune system armored up like a war vet with fresh juices as its weaponry. Laden with vitamins and minerals, these liquid protectors stand sentinel, guarding your body against diseases and infections.
- **Skin glow-up:** Prepare for a radiant transformation! The vitamins and antioxidants within fresh juices launch a crusade against inflammation and oxidative stress, fostering the emergence of beautiful, clear skin.
- **Toxins, begone:** The juice cleanse isn't just a detox, it's a detox extravaganza! Bid farewell to

toxins and waste, paving the way for a cleaner, healthier you.
- **Digestive siesta:** Grant your digestive system a vacation from the grind of solid foods. It's like a treat for your stomach, making digestion smoother and reducing bloating.

But, and it's a crucial "but," not everyone is cut out for this liquid fiesta. Individuals with underlying health conditions, beware! Before diving into the juicing deep end, consult with the healthcare oracle or a registered dietitian. They wield the wisdom to discern if a juice cleanse is both safe and suitable for your unique constitution. Remember, your body is a temple—treat it with the respect it deserves.

PREPPING FOR THE ULTIMATE CLEANSE

Boogie to the pre-cleanse groove a week before your juicing symphony begins. Time to bid adieu to caffeine, alcohol, and processed food. Instead, roll out the red carpet for fruits and vegetables, your new best friends (*5-day cleanse,* n.d.).

Gear check! Ensure your arsenal is equipped with the juicer, blender, and containers, ready to wage war on toxins and boost your health to celestial levels.

- **A golden rule:** During the cleanse, solid food is a no-go. Brace yourself to embrace a liquid love affair, sipping at least 64 ounces of juice per day (*5-day cleanse*, n.d.).

The day before the grand reboot, savor a farewell feast of fruits and vegetables. Hydrate like it's an oasis in the desert, with water flowing freely.

Get into your chef mode and mix up your magic brews for the upcoming juice party. Seal them in airtight containers, like treasures hidden in vaults.

Solidarity, folks! Solid food is still off the menu. Stick to the liquid diet, indulging in at least 64 ounces of juice. Your body is gearing up for the liquid euphoria that awaits.

Remember, this is your journey into the liquid realm, a cleanse of epic proportions. Buckle up, sip, and soar into the world of revitalization!

PREPARING FOR YOUR THREE-, FIVE-, OR SEVEN-DAY JUICE FEAST

Tackling a three-, five-, or seven-day juice feast requires strategic planning and thoughtful preparation. Whether you choose to purchase pre-made juices or create your own with a juicer, the key to a successful cleanse lies in meticulous groundwork.

Hydration is paramount during a juice cleanse. Stock up on water, whether still or sparkling, to stay quenched throughout the cleanse. Broths and teas can complement your hydration strategy, offering variety and warmth to your liquid repertoire.

When you are prepping for your liquid cleanse, remember it's more than just a routine; it's a structured effort for health and renewal (*5-day cleanse,* n.d.). The stage is set for a variety of flavors, with each sip contributing to a refreshed and revitalized version of yourself.

A THREE-DAY DETOX

Strap in because we're diving into the world of a juice cleanse! Get ready to extract the goodness and detoxify like a pro!

The Cleanse Symphony: A Three-Day Ode to Wellness

A juice cleanse is akin to giving your system a reboot—flushing out toxins, boosting the immune system, and dialing up your health. Now, let's talk schedule (*3-Day,* 2023):

The Sip-by-Sip Sonata: Your Three-Day Juice Schedule

- **8:00 a.m.:** Rise and shine with warm lemon water.
- **9:00 a.m.:** Enter the sweet golden green juice.
- **11:00 a.m.:** Get on the healthy Green Machine Juice Express.

- **1:00 p.m.:** Lunch with the classic beautiful beet juice.
- **3:00 p.m.:** Another round of healthy green machine juice.
- **5:00 p.m.:** Dinner date with the carrot juice blend.
- **Before bed:** Sip into dreamland with herbal laxative tea.

The Prologue: Prep Steps Before the Juicy Tale

Before diving into the juicing symphony, here's your backstage pass (*3-Day*, 2023):

- Pick a time when life's stress takes a backseat.
- Stock up on organic, locally grown fruits and veggies.
- Invest in a mighty juicer for maximum nutrient extraction.
- Plan diverse juice recipes for a rainbow of nutrients.
- Guzzle water and herbal teas to stay refreshed.
- Skip caffeine, alcohol, tobacco, and processed villains.
- Snooze adequately to fuel your body's cleansing magic.
- Gentle exercises keep the vibes high.

The Main Act: The Three-Day Juice Extravaganza

In the heart of the cleanse, keep these golden rules in mind (*3-Day*, 2023):

- Drown toxins—drink at least 64 ounces of water daily.
- Adjust juice intake based on hunger and energy.
- Chew your juices like a pro to boost digestion.
- Post-juice, protect those pearly whites with a brush.
- Rest and avoid stress; your body's working its magic.
- Indulge in relaxation like a wellness monarch.
- Monitor the cleanse effects—weight, mood, glow, and bowels.

The Grand Finale: After the Curtain Falls

As the cleanse curtains close, ease back into reality (*3-Day*, 2023):

- Start with fruits, salads, soups, or smoothies.
- Skip heavy hitters—meat, dairy, gluten—for a week.
- Embrace plant-based vibes with a sprinkle of moderation.
- Keep the juicing affair alive with daily sips or snacks.

- Maintain wellness with exercise, sleep, and stress zen.

Sweet Zen Green Dream Recipe

And now, for the star of the show—your Sweet Zen Green Dream (*3-Day*, 2023):

Ingredients:

- 1 inch piece of ginger
- 1 lemon
- 5 cups of kale
- 2 green apples
- 2 cucumbers
- 4 celery stalks

Directions:

- Wash, chop, and prep the ingredients.
- If they're not organic, peel the lemon and ginger.
- Juice it up! Collect the elixir in a jar or pitcher.
- Stir, sip, and savor. Freshness guaranteed up to 24 hours in the fridge.

There you have it, your ticket to a juicier you! Best of luck on your three-day DIY juice cleanse. Sip, smile, and sparkle!

TESTIMONIAL: MAELYNN D'EVREUX

Enter the vibrant world of MaeLynn d'Evreux as she recounts her extraordinary three-day juice cleanse, inspired by the wisdom of esteemed reporter Jaime Stathis (Stathis, 2023). Fueled by a determination to reset her sugar and coffee habits, shed excess weight, and infuse her life with newfound energy, MaeLynn carefully curated a delightful array of juices and smoothies. With unwavering commitment, she adhered faithfully to their recommended drinking schedule.

The inaugural day presented challenges—hunger pangs, fatigue, and the conspicuous absence of her morning coffee ritual. Wrestling with a longing for solid food, MaeLynn confronted a mild headache and bloating. Undaunted, she prioritized hydration with water and herbal tea, redirecting her focus to engaging activities.

Day two marked a positive turning point. MaeLynn felt increasingly alert and invigorated, relishing the flavors and vibrant hues of the juices, especially the green elixirs featuring kale, spinach, celery, cucumber, apple, lemon, and ginger. Notably, her skin adopted a clearer, brighter complexion.

On the third day, she soared like an eagle—lighter, happier, and brimming with energy. Enhanced sleep quality and an earlier rise contributed to her newfound vitality. A check on the scales revealed a remarkable four-pound weight loss over the cleanse period.

Post-cleanse, MaeLynn reintroduced solid foods methodically, commencing with fruits, salads, soups, and smoothies. Steering clear of meat, dairy, gluten, fried, and processed foods for a week, she seamlessly incorporated juices as snacks or meal replacements. Regular exercise, ample sleep, and stress management became cornerstones of her sustained healthy lifestyle.

Thrilled with the outcomes, her three-day juice cleanse severed her sugar and coffee addiction, facilitated weight loss, improved skin and digestion, fortified her immune system, and reshaped her perspective on food choices. This transformative experience heightened her awareness of the profound connection between nutrition and overall well-being.

MaeLynn enthusiastically extends her recommendation for a three-day juice cleanse to those embarking on a detox journey, pursuing health milestones, or simply craving a novel experience (Stathis, 2023). She sagely advises consulting a healthcare professional beforehand, particularly for individuals with medical conditions or those on medications. She cleverly points out that a juice cleanse isn't a magic potion for instant fixes but more like a glam squad for your transition phase—a VIP pass to a sustained, healthier lifestyle.

FIVE-DAY FEAST

Have you decided that you are ready to undertake a five-day juice cleanse? Let's make it a delightful experience. Consider this suggested routine to infuse a bit of zest into your cleanse (*5-Day juice plan*, 2013):

- Start your day with a splash—wake up and relish a large glass of water infused with the zing of lemon. Refreshing, isn't it?
- Before diving into the day, hydrate yourself a bit more—another invigorating glass of water before breakfast sets the tone.
- For your morning feast, embrace a generous glass of vibrant juice. Let the burst of flavors be your wake-up call.
- When the magic of the day unfolds, enjoy your juices at regular two-hour intervals. Sip slowly, relishing every drop like it's the secret liquid of life.

For those who find diving straight into a juice feast challenging, introducing some solid healthy foods might ease the transition (*5-Day juice plan*, 2013):

- Elevate simplicity with sliced cucumbers adorned with lemon and Himalayan sea salt, a crisp, tangy delight.

BEGINNER'S GUIDE TO JUICING | 85

- Delight in a bowl of leafy greens, a verdant bowl of goodness.
- Fancy a fruity rendezvous? Fresh fruit skewers beckon, featuring bananas, apples, and strawberries—nature's candy.
- Dip into the wholesome combo of veggies and hummus—a savory treat for the taste buds.
- Warm your cleanse-infused soul with broth-based soups—a comforting sip between juice intervals.
- If you're in the mood for a dance of flavors, whip up smoothies with a medley of fruits, vegetables, and water—a symphony of freshness.

SEVEN-DAY FEAST

For a harmonious seven-day juice performance, let's craft a schedule that sings with flavor (Walsh, 2021):

- **8:00 a.m.:** Begin your day with the refreshing melody of warm water with lemon.
- **10:00 a.m.:** Let the verdant symphony commence with the Green juice.
- **12:00 p.m.:** The midday crescendo brings you the vibrant Red juice.
- **2:00 p.m.:** Dive into the citrusy serenade of Orange juice.
- **4:00 p.m.:** Rejoin the Green ensemble for another invigorating performance.

- **6:00 p.m.:** The Red juice returns, adding its notes to your flavorful composition.
- **8:00 p.m.:** As the day winds down, savor the soothing Green juice.

Fuel your juicing adventure with these enchanting recipes:

- **Green juice:** Kale, spinach, cucumber, celery, lemon, and a hint of ginger—it's a dance of freshness.
- **Red juice:** Beetroot, carrot, apple, and a dash of ginger—it's a melody of earthy sweetness.
- **Orange juice:** Carrot, orange, and a touch of ginger—it's a citrusy symphony.
- **Lemon water:** Lemon and water.

Writing Down Your Recipes

Whether in a cherished notebook or on a recipe card, document your recipes for effortless and enjoyable repetition.

Writing Down Your Grocery List

To orchestrate this juicing symphony, ensure your kitchen is stocked with the essentials (Walsh, 2021):

- kale
- spinach

- cucumber
- celery
- lemon
- ginger
- beetroot
- carrot
- apple
- turmeric
- grapefruit
- parsley
- dates
- oranges

May your seven-day juice plan be a harmonious and delicious melody!

SETTING EXPECTATIONS

When I finally got over my first detox nightmare, I decided to try it again and did a three-day detox. I tried it not only because I was feeling sluggish and bloated after a vacation but also because that little voice inside kept telling me, "You can do this!"

Surprisingly, I completed my three-day detox and dealt with the side effects like a boss! Amped up and exuding confidence, I decided to try a juicing feast for seven days.

The first day was not too bad. I made myself a green juice with kale, celery, cucumber, apple, and lemon. It tasted fresh and tangy, and I felt proud of myself for making a healthy choice. I drank water and herbal tea throughout the day and had another juice for lunch and dinner. I was hungry but not starving. I thought, "This is easy. I can do this."

The second day was harder. I woke up with a headache and a bad mood. I craved coffee and toast, but I forced myself to drink another green juice. I drank more water and tea, hoping to flush out the toxins from my body. I had another juice for lunch and dinner, but I couldn't finish them. I felt weak and irritable. I thought, "This is awful. Why am I doing this?"

The third day was the worst. I felt completely drained of all my energy. I had no energy, no motivation, no appetite. I contemplated throwing in the towel. Then I remembered what someone in a documentary had said: "You have to set realistic expectations. Don't expect miracles in a week. Just focus on taking one step at a time, and you'll see results in the end." I decided to stick with it, hoping that things would get better.

The fourth day was a turning point. I felt a surge of energy and clarity. I enjoyed my juice, which tasted sweet and refreshing. I felt lighter, more alert, and more positive. I noticed that my skin looked clearer and brighter, and my clothes fit better. I thought, "This is amazing. It's working."

The fifth day was even better. I felt like a new person. I had more energy than ever, and I felt happy and confident. I loved my juice, which tasted like nectar from heaven. I felt satisfied and nourished and didn't miss solid food at all. I thought, "This is incredible. I'm glowing."

The sixth day was the best. I felt like Wonder Woman. I had unlimited energy, creativity, and enthusiasm. I loved my juice, which tasted like liquid gold. I felt full and fulfilled and didn't need anything else. I thought, "This is unbelievable. I'm flying."

The seventh day was the end. I had completed my juicing detox, and I felt fantastic. I had lost weight, gained vitality, and improved my skin condition. I thanked my husband for motivating me during this wonderful experience and thanked myself for sticking with it. I thought, "This is awesome. I did it. I had realized my goal!"

WHY YOU SHOULD SET EXPECTATIONS

Your fitness journey is a series of intentional steps, just like a carefully planned dance. Setting expectations is crucial as it acts as a blueprint, guiding each action to ensure maximum benefit. Think of these benefits (Delgado, 2023):

1. **Mapping the route:** Setting expectations is like plotting the course of your dance. It dictates the

flow, ensuring every workout aligns with your goals.
2. **Staying focused:** Consider each fitness goal as a performance highlight. These expectations keep you directed, ensuring your journey progresses seamlessly.
3. **Recognizing achievements:** Every met expectation signifies progress. They are milestones that reflect your commitment and progress.
4. **Adapting as needed:** As with any skill, the journey may require adjustments. Just as a dancer refines their moves, your fitness routine may need tweaks for optimal results.
5. **Maintaining balance:** In both dance and fitness, equilibrium is vital. Expectations help maintain a steady pace, ensuring holistic well-being.

When it comes to juicing, setting realistic and positive expectations is your guide. They act as a roadmap, directing your journey and keeping you on course. It's all about consistency, including taking small sips regularly and reaching your goals. These gradual steps are more effective than hurried leaps. To sum it up, as you delve into your juicing adventure, let these expectations be your trusted guide.

EIGHT- TO FOURTEEN-DAY JUICE FEAST: PROFESSIONAL JUICE FEASTERS ONLY

So, you've been wading through the juicy wonders of health for a good while now—mastering those shorter cleanses and basking in the glow-up of your well-being. Now, the question looms: Are you ready for the grand detox adventure?

Before the Cleanse: Prep Like a Pro

An eight- to fourteen-day juice feast isn't tailored for beginners. A two-week-long juicing experience can become a physical and emotional rollercoaster. You should anticipate past injuries or health issues making a cameo. But remember, any discomfort is just temporary.

Start with a gastrointestinal cleanse and include a parasite cleanse for enhanced detox efforts. It's like setting up the stage for your main act. Also, it's essential to get at least eight hours of sleep nightly. Detox processes are most effective under the cover of darkness (Ding, 2019).

What to Do During the Cleanse

Here are some guidelines to follow during your feast (Ding, 2019):

- **Sip, don't gulp:** Aim for approximately 17-27 ounces (500 to 800 ml) of freshly made juice three

times a day, with additional sips in between meals. It's your daily juicing anthem.
- **Hydration overdrive:** Stay hydrated with at least 70 ounces (2 liters) of water daily, on top of juices and broths. It's like giving your body a refreshing encore.
- **Juice variety show:** During this extended cleanse, focus on sustaining detox processes with a variety of juices. Beetroots for liver support take the stage but keep the spotlight on healing green juices for digestive and tissue/cell repair.

What to Do After the Juice Feast

Here are some tips and expectations for after your feast (Ding, 2019):

- Gradual weight loss, reduced sugar cravings, increased energy levels—it's your post-cleanse red carpet moment.
- Improved digestion, relief of chronic issues—it's the encore your body deserves.
- Enhanced focus and clearer thoughts, better sleep quality—cheers for your heightened mental clarity.
- Clearer skin—it's your body's way of saying, "I woke up like this."

NAVIGATING THE EPIC: A 15- TO 21-DAY DETOX/JUICE CLEANSE

These detoxes and cleanses are strictly for pro juice feasters only! If you lack a few months of juicing experience, including short and medium cleanses, or if you aim to heal a chronic issue, think twice unless supervised by a qualified natural healer.

What To Do Pre-Feast

Just like the two-week cleanse, you should begin with a gastrointestinal cleanse and a parasite cleanse during the first week. It's like tuning your instrument before a grand performance. It's wise to prioritize sleep, ensuring at least 8 hours nightly for optimal healing. It's your backstage pass to wellness. Additionally, consider a break from supplements, except for probiotics and omega-3 fish oil or flaxseed oil. Coconut oil during an extended fast is recommended. It's your supplement solo (Ding, 2019).

What To Do During the 15- to 21-Day Cleanse

Initial days involve a rough adaptation period and noticeable withdrawal symptoms from unhealthy foods. The first week focuses on superficial detox, healing minor health issues, and addressing acute conditions.

Continuing into the second week intensifies the cleansing process, addressing old injuries and traumas. It's like the gripping climax of your wellness saga.

The third week tends to be calmer, marked by mental clarity and mindfulness. Energy levels may fluctuate, but it's part of the body's process of healing deep injuries.

It's essential to listen to your body. Aim for approximately 17-27 ounces (500 to 800 ml) of freshly made juice three times a day, with occasional sips in between meals. It's the melody of your detox symphony. Just like all other juice feasts, remember to maintain attention to water intake, aiming for at least 70 ounces daily on top of juices, broths, and herbal teas. It's the hydration harmony supporting your body's healing process.

- **Pro tip:** Provide essential vitamins for healing. Include beetroots and other fruits, as suggested in the provided juice recipes. It's like composing a masterpiece for your health (Ding, 2019).

What To Expect After the Extended Feast

Opting for a 21-day detox/juice cleanse signifies a commitment to reaching organs and systems affected by chronic pathologies. This extended period aims to restore balance and heal injuries and damage from earlier years.

In conclusion, whether you're on an 8- to 14-day juice cleanse or the extended 15- to 21-day detox symphony, remember, you're the maestro of your wellness journey. Sip, savor, and let the juicing saga continue!

In this chapter, we went on the wild ride of juice cleansing —a quirky expedition to rejuvenate both body and spirit. From deciphering the secret language of juice cleanses to executing vital steps in preparation, planning, and setting expectations, we've set the stage for a detox that's not just effective but also entertaining.

Maneuvering through the maze of short-, medium-, and long-term cleanses, we discovered challenges, triumphs, and moments that will make your well-being do a happy dance.

KEY TAKEAWAYS

- **Decoding juice cleanses:** Understanding the mystical powers of kale and beets is crucial for short-term detoxification and health enhancement.
- **Pre-detox preparations:** Timing is everything, especially when your juicer becomes your new best friend. And yes, quality matters, both in friendships and juicers.
- **Strategic planning:** Scheduling and setting expectations. It's like orchestrating a juice symphony but with more cucumber and less trombone.
- **Detox reality:** Turns out, that a juice cleanse is a lot like a roller coaster. There are highs, lows, and moments when you question your life choices.

As we shimmy into the next chapter, get ready for a smorgasbord of concoctions tailored to diverse tastes, preferences, and health goals. From eye-opening morning blends to nightcap elixirs that could moonlight as your new favorite party drink. These recipes are here to tickle your taste buds and add a dash of pizzazz to your journey to becoming a healthier, more vibrant you.

Let the blending and the juicing begin!

Juice Up Their Journey With Your Review!

Spread the Zest of Health and Happiness

"True happiness comes from helping others, and what's sweeter than the ripest fruit."

— JADE JUICE

Hey there, amazing juice explorer! Did you know that by doing something small, you can create a big ripple of goodness? If we have the chance to spread a little joy and health, we should grab it with both hands!

So, here's a little question for you...

Would you be willing to help a fellow juice buddy, someone you've never met, without expecting anything in return?

Who is this mystery person? They're a lot like you were once – eager to start their juicy journey, looking to make a change, and searching for the right guidance.

Our goal is to make the wonders of juicing accessible to everyone. Everything I do is driven by this mission. And the best way to achieve this is by reaching... well, everyone!

This is where you, my fabulous juicing friend, come in. Most people decide on a book based on its cover and what others say about it. So, here's my big ask for a fellow juicing beginner you haven't met:

Could you please help them by leaving a review for this book?

Your thoughtful review doesn't cost a dime and takes less than a minute, but it can make a world of difference. Your words could help…

...another family discover the joy of healthy living.
...someone else find their path to better energy and focus.
...a newbie experience the thrill of weight loss and better sleep.
...another dreamer feel empowered and inspired.
...one more person transform their life through juicing.

To spread this joy and make a real difference, it's super simple and quick:

Just leave a review.

Scan this QR code to share your thoughts:

If the thought of helping someone out there makes your heart happy, you're definitely my kind of person. Welcome to the club! You're now a part of our juicy family.

I can't wait to help you achieve amazing energy, focus, and health gains faster and easier than you ever imagined. The juicy tips and tricks in the next chapters are going to blow your mind!

Thank you from the bottom of my fruit basket. Now, let's get back to our exciting juicy adventure!

Your biggest cheerleader,
Jade Juice

P.S. - Fun fact: When you share something valuable with someone, it makes you invaluable to them. If you think this book will help another juicing enthusiast like yourself, why not share it with them? Let's spread the juicy goodness together!

5

JUICING RECIPES FOR YOUR NEEDS

As you've traversed the pages of this juicing odyssey, you've ventured into a world where vibrant concoctions transform not just glasses but lives. Each chapter has unfolded testimonies of triumph, unveiling the profound impact of juicing on the lives of everyday people just like you.

In a world where fruit and veggies reign supreme, juicers become the silent achievers of super health transformations. I'd like to introduce you to some incredible folks whose lives have taken a jaw-dropping turn, all thanks to the power of juicing (*Success stories*, 2021):

- Aaron, once grappling with the weight of 42 extra pounds, found solace in the vibrant elixirs that not only shredded the excess baggage but turned his terrifying liver scans into a masterpiece of "perfect." From hospital beds to juicing feasts, Aaron's journey unveils the magic of changing diets and healing livers.

- Barbara, having bid adieu to 30 stubborn pounds, not only discovered a newfound love for veggies but triumphed over sugar and processed food addiction. In her own words, juicing became the secret to unlocking boundless energy and confidence that radiates from the inside out.
- Crissy, shedding 25 pounds and waving farewell to high blood pressure, conquered her fear of fruits and vegetables with a juicing adventure that extended beyond the kitchen. Her story is a testament to the transformative power of sipping on nature's goodness, paving the way for a more adventurous lifestyle.
- AJ, with a victorious battle against insomnia and 20 pounds left in its wake, shares how juicing became her remedy for chronic pain and stress. A tranquil night's sleep, once a distant dream, became her reality—all without the aid of medication.
- And then there's Adam, a triumphant weight loss warrior who bid farewell to a staggering 140 pounds and a binge eating disorder. Through the alchemy of juicing, he rewrote his story with food, self-love, and restored liver function. His journey is a guiding light for people seeking transformation on a larger scale.

These testimonials I have included are not meant to intimidate but to inspire. They are not unattainable dreams but invitations to a reality where juicing becomes a seamless part of your life. The road might have its hitches and snags, but remember, every marathon is made of individual steps, and every sip is a victory.

The recipes and tips offered in this book are not just instructions; they are your companions on this voyage. Every ingredient, every blend, is a small yet significant step toward a healthier, more vibrant version of yourself.

DIGESTION AND GUT HEALTH

Having struggled with irritable bowel syndrome for an extended period, I found solace in juice feasting when conventional remedies proved ineffective. The transformation was remarkable—bloating and cramps became things of the past, replaced by a newfound sense of regularity and energy. Additionally, my skin cleared up, and the stiffness in my joints noticeably diminished.

Fatigue, sluggishness, and weight management challenges were persistent monkeys on my back. The introduction of a juicier lifestyle sparked a positive change. Surprisingly delectable juices became a delightful addition to my routine, and their ease of preparation was a pleasant surprise. Within a few weeks, the impact was evident—I felt more vibrant and lighter than a feather. Improved digestion and a reduction in cravings were among the notable benefits, marking a significant shift in my overall well-being.

My juicy voyage not only provided a solution for my gut health woes but also introduced a palate-pleasing and convenient approach to nutrition. If you, too, seek to revitalize your health and well-being, consider the potential transformative effects of incorporating juices into your daily regimen.

If you want to start juicing for gut health, here are some juicy recipes that you can try:

Fanta Green Applicious

Indulge in the fruity and refreshing symphony of this vibrant juice, reminiscent of a healthier take on the classic Fanta Green Apple soda. Beyond its delightful taste, this concoction serves as a powerhouse of nutrition. Packed with vitamin C and antioxidants, it acts as a formidable defender, shielding your cells from potential damage and inflammation.

The inclusion of green apples not only enhances sweetness but also contributes valuable fiber, offering a delectable feast for your gut bacteria. Meanwhile, the zesty touch of lemon juice not only adds another layer of invigorating flavor but is also essential in maintaining the optimal pH balance in your body.

So, sip away on this invigorating blend that not only tantalizes your taste buds but also nourishes your body with a burst of goodness (Frey, 2023):

Serving Size: 12 oz

Ingredients:

- 1/2 cup of pineapple chunks
- 1 1/4 apples
- 1/4 of a lemon
- 2 1/2 stalks of celery
- 2 cups of kale
- 1 thumb size of ginger

Directions:

1. Wash all ingredients.
2. Chop the celery, kale, and ginger into pieces.
3. Peel and remove the pineapple's crown (unless organic).
4. Cut the pineapple and apple into chunks.
5. Peel and cut the lemon.
6. Run everything through a juicer and enjoy!

Green Inflammation Buster

Immerse yourself in the invigorating experience of this crisp and perfectly balanced drink. Refreshing to the core, this blend is not just a delight for the senses, but it is also a nutritional powerhouse. Brimming with antioxidants, it acts as a detoxifying agent, diligently working to rid your body of toxins and combat inflammation.

Kale and spinach take center stage, bringing with them the green goodness of chlorophyll. This vital component plays a pivotal role in cleansing your blood and supporting the liver, making each sip a step towards rejuvenating your internal systems. Adding to the hydrating prowess of this mixture, celery and cucumber, rich in water content, work harmoniously to replenish your body's fluids and facilitate the flushing out of toxins.

Let's not forget the zesty twist—lemon juice. Beyond its vibrant flavor, it delivers a surge of vitamin C, which has been shown to strengthen the immune system. Additionally, it contributes to balancing the pH levels of your body, promoting an alkaline environment for optimal well-being.

Serving Size: 12 oz

Ingredients:

- 2 cups of spinach
- 2 celery stalks
- 1 cucumber
- 1 lemon
- 1 inch piece of ginger
- 1 apple
- 1 cup of chunked pineapple

Directions:

1. Measure and clean the ingredients.
2. Chop the ginger, celery, and spinach.
3. Cut the apple and cucumber into chunks.
4. Cut the pineapple into chunks after peeling and cutting away the green crown.
5. Cut the lemon into four parts without removing the skin, then press.
6. For those without a press, the skins may be removed and juiced with the other ingredients.
7. Juice everything together (Frey, 2023).

Revitalize and Restore Aloe Vera Elixir

At the heart of this drink lies the miraculous aloe vera gel, boasting polysaccharides that go beyond mere flavor, working to renew and repair your gut lining. Say goodbye to digestive woes as this juice plays the star role in the healing process.

The delightful and juicy honeydew melon steps into the spotlight, infusing the blend with its hydrating powers. A burst of refreshment awaits as you sip on the high-water content, bidding farewell to toxins while embracing essential hydration for your body. It's not just a drink; it's a revitalizing ritual for your digestive well-being. And let's not overlook the zesty contributor—lime juice.

Together, these elements create a harmonious symphony that not only tantalizes your taste buds but also provides a therapeutic touch to your digestive system.

Serving Size: 6-8 oz

Ingredients:

- 1/4 of a lime
- 1/4 cup of honeydew melon
- 2 tablespoons of pure aloe vera juice
- 3 1/2 tablespoons of coconut water

Directions:

1. Wash and peel the honeydew melon and lime.
2. Cut the lime in half and squeeze the juice into a measuring cup.
3. Add the aloe vera gel and the coconut water, then stir well.
4. Run everything through a juicer (Frey, 2023).

Ginger Turmeric Gut Doctor

Elevate your immunity and quell inflammation with this mighty juice shot, a potent elixir designed to pack a punch against pain and swelling. With ginger and turmeric, you have formidable anti-inflammatories ready to go to battle for your well-being.

Ginger steps in with its zesty kick, known for being an inflammation buster. Meanwhile, turmeric, with its golden hue, brings its powerhouse compound, curcumin, to the forefront.

Lemon juice adds vitamin C and helps alkalize your body. Curcumin, the active element in turmeric, is better absorbed when it is combined with black pepper.

Serving Size: 8 oz

Ingredients:

- 3 inches of ginger (chopped)
- 1 lemon
- 1 celery stalk
- a pinch of black pepper per serving
- a pinch of cayenne pepper per serving
- 2 apples

Directions:

1. Wash and peel the lemon.
2. Cut the apple into chunks.
3. Chop the celery and ginger into pieces.
4. Run them through a juicer.
5. To each shot, add a sprinkle of cayenne and black pepper (Frey, 2023).

Carrotty Pineapplicious Brew

Indulge in the delightful symphony of sweetness and tanginess with this refreshing juice that not only tantalizes your taste buds but also offers a boost to your well-being. Packed with vitamin C, it's your go-to drink for fortifying the immune system and combating inflammation.

Carrots take the spotlight, bringing their vibrant orange hue and a hefty dose of beta-carotene to the mix. This powerhouse antioxidant stands guard against oxidative stress, offering protection to your precious cells.

Adding to the citrusy goodness, orange juice steps in as a key player. Bursting with vitamin C it not only contributes to immune boosting but also plays a pivotal role in collagen production. Your skin and connective tissues will thank you for this extra dose of support.

Serving Size: 12 oz

Ingredients:

- 1 lime
- 3 carrots
- 4 cups of pineapple chunks
- 2 oranges
- 1 inch ginger root

Directions:

1. Wash and chop the carrots and ginger roots.
2. Cut the lime into four parts and do not remove the skin, then press. For those without a press, the skins may be removed and juiced with the other ingredients.
3. Peel the oranges and chop off the pineapple crown.
4. Run everything through a juicer (Frey, 2023).

Tangy Beet Cucumber Gut Fuel

This juice has a delicious fruity flavor with a hint of earthiness, and it's loaded with nutrients that can help increase blood flow and reduce inflammation. Beetroot nitrates can help expand blood vessels and improve circulation to the intestines.

Bromelain, an enzyme with anti-inflammatory effects, is found in pineapple. Oranges are rich in vitamin C, which might help your immune system.

Serving Size: 12 oz

Ingredients:

- A handful of kale
- 1 cucumber
- 2 beetroots
- 1 orange

Directions:

1. Clean and measure ingredients.
2. Cut the cucumber into chunks.
3. Peel the oranges and chop off the tops of the beets.
4. Then, chop the kale into pieces.
5. Run all the ingredients through a juicer.

Zesty Citrus Root Beer

This juice isn't just a juice; it's a symphony of nutrients working in harmony to nurture your gut and combat inflammation. Carrots take center stage, not just for their natural sweetness but also for their high fiber content. A gut-friendly ally, they promote the growth of good bacteria, ensuring your digestive system stays in top-notch condition.

Apples join the party, bringing along their secret weapon—pectin. This unique fiber isn't only an indulgence for your gustatory senses; it's also a buffet for your gut bacteria, providing the food they require. Rich in vitamin C, lemon juice helps encourage the stomach's production of digestive juices. As a natural anti-inflammatory, ginger can help calm the lining of your stomach.

Serving Size: 12 oz

Ingredients:

- 7 large carrots

- 1 apple
- 1 lemon
- 1 1/3 inches of ginger

Directions:

1. Ingredients should be weighed and cleaned.
2. Chop the carrots, apples, and ginger into chunks.
3. Cut the lemon in four parts and don't remove the skin, then press. For those without a press, the skins may be removed and juiced with the other ingredients.
4. Juice everything together and enjoy (Frey, 2023).

Orchard Fresh Cucumber Blend

This blend is a gut-friendly juice with cucumber, apple, lemon, celery, and ginger. It is crisp and refreshing, with a touch of spice that can help improve your digestion and reduce inflammation.

Serving Size: 12 oz

Ingredients:

- 1 cucumber
- 1 apple
- 1 lemon
- 2 celery stalks
- 2 inches of ginger

Directions:

1. Peel and chop the ginger.
2. Wash the celery and chop it thoroughly.
3. Core the apple and cut it into quarters.
4. Cut the lemon into wedges with the peel on after washing it thoroughly.
5. Wash the cucumber and cut it into pieces (Frey, 2023).
6. Put the cucumber pieces, apple quarters, lemon wedges, celery pieces, and ginger chunks into the juicer and juice until smooth.

In conclusion, these digestion-friendly recipes offer a delightful blend of flavors while promoting a healthy gut. From soothing herbal infusions to nutrient-packed smoothies, each recipe contributes to digestive well-being. Feel free to explore, mix, and match to find your perfect digestive miracle.

Cheers to good digestion and a happy belly!

ENERGY

Plunge into the invigorating world of juicing, where the transformative effects extend beyond shedding pounds—energizing and revitalizing juice feasters. Countless juice enthusiasts have shared the profound impact juicing has had on their lives, creating a tapestry of vibrant well-being.

Renowned Reboot Naturopath Claire Georgiou says in the hustle and bustle of her clients' daily lives, some used to return home feeling drained and fatigued (Georgiou, 2015). The prospect of preparing a quick, healthy dinner felt like an insurmountable challenge, leaving them barely able to muster the energy to crawl into bed. However, the introduction of juicing sparked a remarkable shift. The narrative changed, and they found themselves amazed by the newfound vitality that permeated their lives.

No longer confined by exhaustion, Claire claims many of her patients discovered an enhanced capacity to engage in activities during their spare time or on weekends. It was as if they had acquired a new lease on life. Witnessing this transformation consistently brings a smile to her face, and she finds herself cheering for her patients' newfound vigor.

For those incorporating one or two juices into their balanced daily diet, the impact on energy levels becomes apparent within a few short weeks. However, for those embarking on a juice-only Reboot, the boost is even more immediate, often manifesting within a span of just a few days, says Claire (Georgiou, 2015).

Juicing acts as a catalyst for a surge in energy, offering us the vitality to accomplish more and savor life's moments.

The testimonies of those who have embraced juicing echo a sentiment of revitalization and a rekindled zest for life.

Consider adding one or two juices per day to your lifestyle, and you'll witness a notable difference in your energy levels within a matter of weeks.

Juicing is more than a dietary choice; it's a gateway to a vibrant and energized way of life. It's a journey that not only aids in shedding pounds but, more importantly, transforms the way we experience and embrace life.

Beet Street Boogie

The Beet Street Boogie is an energy-boosting juice with celery, apples, beetroot, cucumber, lemon, orange, and strawberries. This juice is colorful and delicious, with a mix of flavors that can help fight off infections and inflammation like a SWAT team (*11 energizing,* n.d.).

Serving Size: 16-20 oz

Ingredients:

- 1 1/2 cups whole strawberries
- 1 lemon
- 6 medium carrots
- 1 cucumber
- 2 apples
- 1 beet
- 1 orange
- 1 stalk of celery

Directions:

1. Wash the celery and chop it into pieces.
2. Core the apple and cut it into quarters.
3. Wash the beetroot and cut it into pieces.
4. Wash the carrots and cut them into pieces.
5. Wash the cucumber and cut it into pieces.
6. Cut the lemon into wedges.
7. Peel the orange and cut it into segments.
8. Wash and hull the strawberries.
9. Put the celery pieces, apple quarters, beetroot pieces, carrot pieces, cucumber pieces, lemon wedges, orange segments, and strawberry halves into the juicer.

Pear Citrus Fusion

Delight in the velvety fusion of pear, lemon, banana, and ginger. This juice orchestrates a delicate balance between subtle sweetness and zesty notes, heightened by the creamy texture of banana and the invigorating kick of ginger.

Beyond its delightful flavor, this fusion of flavors holds the potential to refresh your liver and contribute to radiant skin. As you savor each sip, let this mild and smooth blend seamlessly integrate into your wellness routine (*11 energizing,* n.d.).

JADE JUICE

Serving Size: 6-8 oz

Ingredients:

- 1 inch of ginger
- 1 banana
- 1/2 lemon
- 1 pear

Directions:

1. Peel the banana and cut it into pieces.
2. Peel and chop the ginger.
3. Wash the pear and cut it into slices.
4. Cut the lemon into wedges.
5. Put the pear slices, lemon wedges, and ginger chunks into the juicer.
6. Pour the juice and the banana into a blender and blend until smooth.
7. Pour the fusion into a glass and enjoy chilled over ice (optional).

Citrus Glow

Sip your way to weight-loss success with this low-calorie, high-fiber juice boasting vitamin C and calcium. A satisfying blend designed to keep you feeling full and content, it's not just a drink; it's a step towards your health and wellness goals (*11 energizing,* n.d.). Embrace the goodness! Embrace the journey!

Serving Size: 12 oz

Ingredients:

- 1/3 cup of bok choy
- 1 orange
- 1 banana

Directions:

1. Wash the bok choy and chop it into parts.
2. Peel the bananas and oranges and cut them into slices.
3. Put the orange slices, bok choy, and orange juice into the juicer.
4. Mix the juice with the banana in a blender and blend until smooth.
5. Sip and enjoy chilled!

Zesty Delight

A cleansing juice with lemon, banana, and pear. This juice is light and creamy, with a hint of sourness that can help balance your pH levels, raise your energy, and flush out toxins (*11 energizing,* n.d.).

Serving Size: 8-12 oz

Ingredients:

- 1 lemon

- 1 banana
- 2 cups of sliced pears

Directions:

1. Wash the pears and cut them into slices.
2. Peel the banana and cut it into pieces.
3. Cut the lemon into wedges.
4. Put the pear slices and lemon wedges into the juicer and juice up a storm.
5. Put the banana pieces in a blender and pour the juice over.
6. Blend everything until smooth.

Martha Stewart's Potion

This juice is one of Martha Stewart's favorites. It's a wake-up juice with grapefruits, carrots, and ginger. This juice is tart and spicy, with a burst of vitamin C and beta-carotene that can help you start your day with a bang (*11 energizing*, n.d.).

Serving Size: 12 oz

Ingredients:

- 1 inch of ginger
- 5 small carrots
- 2 grapefruits

Directions:

1. Peel and chop the ginger.
2. Wash the carrots and cut them into pieces.
3. Cut the grapefruits in half and squeeze out the juice.
4. Put the grapefruit juice, carrot pieces, and ginger chunks into the juicer.

Berry O'Bomber

Revitalize your energy levels with this fatigue-fighting potion. Crafted with the goodness of white grape, kiwi, strawberry, and lemon, it's a sweet and tangy symphony that delivers a burst of vitamin C and antioxidants (*11 energizing,* n.d.).

Stay alert! Stay energized! Sip your way to vitality!

Serving Size: 12 oz

Ingredients:

- 2 cups of whole strawberries
- 1 cup of kiwi
- 1 lemon
- 1 1/2 cups of grapes (white)

Directions:

1. Wash the grapes and remove the stems.

2. Peel the kiwi and cut it into pieces.
3. Wash and hull the strawberries.
4. Cut the lemon into wedges.
5. Put the grapes, kiwi, strawberries, and lemon into the juicer.
6. Enjoy with or without ice!

Popeye's Redbull

Dive into the refreshing embrace of this sweet and green concoction, blending the tropical notes of pineapple with the wholesome goodness of kale and spinach. Beyond the delightful taste, this juice boasts a powerful combination of chlorophyll, vitamin K, and iron, working harmoniously to fortify your bones and invigorate your blood.

Take a sip, revel in the vibrant flavors, and let the nourishment unfold (*11 energizing,* n.d.).

Serving Size: 12-16 oz

Ingredients:

- A handful of kale
- 2 inches of ginger
- A handful of spinach
- 1/2 a lemon
- 1/4 of pineapple

Directions:

1. Cut the pineapple into chunks.
2. Wash the kale and remove the stems.
3. Wash the spinach and pat it dry.
4. Peel and chop the lemon and ginger, if using.
5. Put the pineapple chunks, kale leaves, spinach leaves, and lemon and ginger pieces into the juicer.

Orang'ya Glad Carrot Brew

A stress-relieving juice with oranges, lemon, carrots, and ginger. This juice is sweet and sour, with a kick of ginger that can help calm your nerves and boost your mood (*11 energizing*, n.d.).

Serving Size: 16 oz

Ingredients:

- 2 inches of ginger
- 4 carrots
- 1 lemon
- 2 oranges

Directions:

1. Wash the carrots and cut them into pieces.
2. Peel and chop the ginger.

3. Peel the oranges and cut them into segments.
4. Cut the lemon into wedges.
5. Put the orange segments, lemon wedges, carrot pieces, and ginger chunks into the juicer.

Green Machine Booster

Elevate your game with this powerhouse juice featuring kale, apple, orange, cucumber, and ginger. Packed with antioxidants, vitamins, minerals, and enzymes, it's your go-to drink for cleansing, digestion, and an immunity boost. Embrace the vibrant blend and let your body revel in the goodness (*11 energizing,* n.d.).

Serving Size: 12 oz

Ingredients:

- 1 inch of ginger
- 1 cucumber
- 1 orange
- 2 cups of kale
- 2 apples

Directions:

1. Wash the kale and remove the stems.
2. Core the apple and cut it into quarters.
3. Peel the orange and cut it into segments.
4. Wash the cucumber and cut it into pieces.

5. Peel and chop the ginger.
6. Put the kale, apple, orange, cucumber, and ginger into the juicer and juice away.
7. Enjoy over ice!

Tropical Pom-Orange Burst

Quench your thirst and energize your day with this revitalizing juice bursting with vitamin C, potassium, and folate. Tailor-made for a hot summer day or any moment when you crave a refreshing pick-me-up, this life-saver is here to elevate your energy levels and delight your taste buds (*11 energizing*, n.d.).

So, why settle for ordinary when you can sip on a glass of extraordinary vitality? Pour, sip, and let the goodness flow!

Serving Size: 12 oz

Ingredients:

- 1 orange
- 1/2 cup of pineapple
- 1 pomegranate

Directions:

1. Cut the pineapple into chunks.
2. Peel the orange and cut it into segments.

3. Chop the pomegranate into quarters, then use a spoon to remove the seeds.
4. Put the pomegranate, orange segments, and pineapple chunks into the juicer and juice until it's smooth.

DETOX

Beyoncé is one of the most famous and successful singers in the world, but she is also known for her dedication to fitness and health. She has tried various methods of detoxing and cleansing her body, including using juices. One of the most popular juice detoxes that Beyoncé has followed is the Master Cleanse, which she used to lose "20 pounds in two weeks for her role in *Dreamgirls* in 2006," according to *USA Today* (Ali, 2019).

The Master Cleanse is a juice feast that consists of drinking a wide array of juices containing ginger, lemon juice, turmeric, maple syrup, and cayenne pepper for 10 days without eating any solid food. This cleanse aims to aid in weight loss by eliminating toxins from the body.

Below, you'll find five of the benefits of juice detoxes (Ali, 2019):

1. They can provide a large amount of vitamins, minerals, and antioxidants from fruits and vegetables, which can boost the immune system,

protect the cells from damage and inflammation, and support skin health.
2. They can help hydrate the body, as juices are mostly water. This added hydration can improve blood circulation, kidney function, digestion, and elimination of waste products.
3. Processed foods, added sugars, coffee, alcohol, and other things that may be harmful to one's health and wellbeing can be lessened with their assistance.
4. After completing the detox program, they can help reset taste receptors and appetites, making it simpler to stick to a healthy diet.
5. They can help improve mood and mental clarity, as some juices contain ingredients that can stimulate the production of serotonin, dopamine, and other neurotransmitters that regulate emotions and cognition.

Here are some great detox recipes:

Toxin Beetdown

This detox juice is a nutritional powerhouse in a glass. It's made with beetroot, carrot, celery, apple, and lemon for a vibrant and super flavorful juice (Beiser, 2023).

Jade Juice

Serving Size: 50 oz

Ingredients:

- 1 lemon
- 1 lime
- 1 lb of beetroot
- 1 cucumber (medium)
- 2 carrots
- 3 apples
- 1 bunch of parsley
- 2 celery stalks

Directions:

1. Peel, cut, and chop the ingredients accordingly.
2. Run them through a juicer.
3. Filter the juice through a cheesecloth.
4. Enjoy.

Ginger Carrot Gold

This detox juice is full of vitamin C and beta-carotene. It's a blend of carrots, oranges, lemon, and ginger for a healthy and delicious juice. Vitamin A, which is abundant in carrots, lowers cholesterol (Beiser, 2023).

Serving Size: 24 oz

Ingredients:

- 4 carrots (large)
- 2 oranges
- 1 lemon
- 1/2 inch of ginger

Directions:

1. Peel and chop the ingredients.
2. Run them through a juicer.
3. Filter the juice through a mesh bag.
4. Add lemon juice and ice.

Pineapple Zinger Bomb

This detox juice is a blend of fresh pineapple, ginger, turmeric, and lime. It has anti-inflammatory, digestive-boosting, and liver-cleansing properties. It's also sweet and refreshing (Beiser, 2023).

Serving Size: 24 oz

Ingredients:

- 1 lime
- 3 cups of pineapple chunks
- 3 pieces of turmeric
- 2 inches of ginger root

Directions:

1. Wash everything thoroughly.
2. Peel and chop off the crown of the pineapple.
3. Cut all the ingredients into chunks.
4. Then, run them through a juicer.
5. Strain if needed and enjoy chilled.

Kale-ifornia Dreamin'

This green juice will help you cleanse your body and boost your immunity with its rich nutrients. It's made with fresh kale, cucumber, Fuji apples, and lemon. You will love this natural detox drink (Beiser, 2023).

Serving Size:

- 12 oz

Ingredients:

- 1 lemon
- 1 cucumber
- 1 bunch of kale leaves
- 2 Fuji apples

Directions:

1. Wash the ingredients thoroughly.
2. Cut the kale into pieces.
3. Chop the cucumber and apples into chunks.
4. Peel the lemon and cut into quarters.
5. Remember, you don't have to remove the lemon peel if you have a cold press.
6. Then, run them through a juicer.
7. Enjoy over ice or chilled.

Pink Panther Detox Juice

This detox juice is a powerful tonic that helps lower blood sugar levels, fight inflammation, improve digestion, and boost energy. It's made with grapefruit, apple cider vinegar and honey (Beiser, 2023).

Serving Size: 12 oz

Ingredients:

- 1 cup of grapefruit juice
- 2 tablespoons of apple cider vinegar
- 1 teaspoon of honey

Directions:

1. Mix all the ingredients in a glass of water.
2. Stir well.

3. Enjoy every sip!

Golden Sweet Elixir

This detox juice is a sweet and refreshing drink that's high in iron, vitamin C, and essential minerals. It's made with pineapple, celery, cucumber, green apple, spinach, ginger, and lemon (*10 best detox*, 2022).

Ingredients:

- 1 handful of parsley
- 1 lemon (medium)
- 1 cup of pineapple chunks
- 2 celery stalks
- 1 cucumber (large)
- 1 green apple (medium)
- 2 cups of spinach leaves
- 1 inch of ginger

Directions:

1. Wash and chop the ingredients.
2. Run them through a juicer.
3. Strain the juice if needed.
4. Drink up.

Cider Cleanse Turmeric Tonic

This detox juice is a powerful tonic that helps lower blood sugar levels, fight inflammation, improve digestion, and boost energy. It's made with apple cider vinegar, turmeric, cayenne pepper, honey, and water (*10 best detox*, 2022).

Serving Size: 16 oz

Ingredients:

- 1 tablespoon of apple cider vinegar
- juice of 1 lemon
- 1/4 teaspoon of turmeric powder
- A pinch of cayenne pepper
- 1 tablespoon of honey
- a cup of water (warm)

Directions:

1. Mix all the ingredients in a glass of water.
2. Stir well.
3. Drink with a straw.

Cilantro Serenade

This detox juice is a refreshing and hydrating drink that tastes like summer. It's made with cilantro leaves, lemon juice, and a sweetener of your choice (*10 best detox*, 2022).

JADE JUICE

Serving Size: 24 oz

Ingredients:

- 3 cups of cilantro leaves
- 1/4 teaspoon salt
- 2 1/2 cups of cold water
- the juice of 4 lemons
- 3 tablespoons of sweetener (such as honey or maple syrup)

Directions:

1. Wash and cut the bottoms of the cilantro.
2. Add the lemon juice, sweetener, salt, and water.
3. Blend all the ingredients in your juicer until smooth.
4. Filter through a sleeve or a fine mesh strainer to remove the pulp.
5. Serve over ice or chilled.

We've delved into a flavorful spectrum of detox juices. From the crisp embrace of kale and cucumber to the soothing melody of honeydew and aloe vera, each concoction is not merely a beverage but a liquid symphony for your well-being.

These juices, rich in antioxidants, vitamins, and minerals, stand as allies in the quest for health. Whether you seek to cleanse, boost immunity, or simply revel in their delicious essence, these preparations beckon you to embrace a fresher, more vibrant you.

As you venture into the realm of these nourishing potions, may your taste buds dance with delight, and your body, mind, and spirit find harmony in the wholesome embrace of these detoxifying brews.

INFLAMMATION

Juicing is a popular way to consume more fruits and vegetables, which are rich in vitamins, minerals, antioxidants, and anti-inflammatory compounds. Juicing can also give your digestive system a break while still providing you with essential nutrients.

However, not all juices are created equal. Some fruits and vegetables have more anti-inflammatory benefits than others, and some combinations can enhance their effects. Next, I will introduce you to some of the best juicing recipes that I personally use to help fight inflammation and heal my body.

Watermelon Basil Sublime

Quench your summer thirst with this hydrating solution that not only embodies the essence of summer but also works wonders to reduce swelling and rehydrate your body. Dive into the refreshing goodness of watermelon, a juicy delight that not only boasts high water content but also houses lycopene, a carotenoid with anti-inflammatory properties that lend a hand in safeguarding your skin from sun damage.

Enter basil, the herbaceous hero that goes beyond flavor. Its presence in this concoction is not just for taste—it brings relief to arthritis symptoms and adds a mood-enhancing touch, making this drink a true tonic for your body and mind (Cole, 2023).

Serving Size: 24 oz

Ingredients:

- 6 basil leaves
- 1 small watermelon
- the juice of 1 lime

Directions:

1. Wash everything.
2. Remove the watermelon seeds and rind.
3. Cut the watermelon into pieces.
4. Add everything together and juice well.
5. Add ice if you like, and enjoy every sip!

Berry White

Skyrocket your vitality with this antioxidant-packed elixir designed not only to tantalize your taste buds but also to amp up your energy and circulation.

Meet the star of the show—blueberries, brimming with anthocyanins, vibrant pigments that not only paint them blue but also wield anti-inflammatory magic.

Beyond their stunning color, these little powerhouses safeguard your brain from aging and give your memory a boost (Cole, 2023).

Serving Size: 18 oz

Ingredients:

- 2 cups of spinach leaves
- 2 cups of blueberries
- 2 apples

Directions:

1. Wash everything thoroughly.
2. Cut apples and spinach.
3. Add everything together and run through the juicer.

Minty Fennel Juice

Delight in the calming embrace of this refreshing juice, designed not only to quench your thirst but also to lend a hand with digestion and infections. Apples take center stage, offering a dual benefit with their antioxidant-rich goodness and fiber content. Apples not only shield your cells from harm but also lend a helping hand to your gut health, ensuring your well-being from the inside out.

Introducing fennel, a vegetable with a delightful licorice-like flavor that goes beyond taste. Its presence in this concoction can assist in alleviating bloating, gas, and cramps, making this drink a soothing remedy for digestive discomfort.

And let's not forget the invigorating touch of mint, an herb that not only adds a burst of freshness to your palate but also works wonders for your stomach. Known for its calming properties, mint can provide relief from digestive woes while leaving your breath minty-fresh (Cole, 2023).

Serving Size: 32 oz

Ingredients:

- 10 oz of spinach
- 1 cucumber
- 1 bulb of fennel
- 2 apples
- half a lemon
- 1 bunch of mint

Directions:

1. Wash all the produce.
2. Chop the cucumber, fennel, spinach, and mint into pieces.

3. Cut the apples into chunks.
4. Peel and cut the lemon.
5. Add everything to the juicer.
6. Enjoy every sip!

The Hulk Queen

Quench your thirst and invigorate your senses with this refreshing juice that doubles as a natural remedy for inflammation and pain. Green apples take the lead, delivering a burst of vitamin C essential for collagen synthesis and wound healing.

Kale, a nutritional powerhouse, adds protein, calcium, iron, and vitamin K to the mix, transforming this drink into a nutrient-packed elixir for your overall well-being. The lively combination of lemon and ginger amplifies both the flavor and health benefits. Rich in additional vitamin C, these ingredients contribute a zesty kick while their anti-inflammatory properties enhance the wellness quotient of the juice.

So, indulge in this revitalizing blend, relishing the crisp taste while nourishing your body with essential nutrients and a built-in defense against inflammation and pain. It's not just a drink; it's a wellness boost in every sip (Cole, 2023).

JADE JUICE

Serving Size: 12 oz

Ingredients:

- 1 bunch of kale
- 1 lemon Wedge
- 1 cup of grapes
- 1 slice of ginger

Directions:

1. Wash everything thoroughly.
2. Chop the ginger into chunks.
3. Add all the ingredients to the juicer and juice away.

Tropical Spice

Indulge in the delightful symphony of flavors that characterize this exceptional juice blend. Its delectable combination of sweetness and a hint of spice not only tantalizes your taste buds but also brings a myriad of health benefits to the table. At its core, pineapple takes center stage, contributing to the powerful enzyme bromelain.

Renowned for its digestive properties, bromelain not only aids in digestion but also supports joint health. Adding to the health-packed ensemble, ginger and turmeric join the party as robust anti-inflammatory spices. Beyond their ability to add a zing to the flavor profile, they offer potential relief from discomfort, assist in alleviating nausea, and even combat infections.

Cinnamon, another noteworthy player, steps in with its blood-sugar-regulating prowess, making it a valuable addition for those mindful of their glucose levels. As if this weren't impressive enough, the juice boasts a supporting cast of other ingredients, each contributing its unique blend of vitamins, minerals, and antioxidants (Cole, 2023).

Serving Size: 32 oz

Ingredients:

- 1 tablespoon of cinnamon powder
- 15 pieces of fresh turmeric root (about 3 inches each)
- 1 pineapple
- 2 cucumbers

Directions:

1. Wash all ingredients thoroughly.
2. Chop the cucumber and turmeric roots into chunks.
3. Peel and cut off the pineapple's crown.
4. Add the cinnamon powder and juice everything together.

These are just some of the juicing recipes that I personally use and that can help you reduce inflammation and improve your health. They are easy to make and taste great. You can drink them regularly or whenever you need a boost of nutrients and anti-inflammatory benefits.

As we wrap up our exploration of inflammation-fighting heroes, we've traversed a flavorful landscape that not only tantalizes the taste buds but also stands as a potent arsenal against inflammation. From the zing of ginger and turmeric to the sweet embrace of berries and citrus, each drink is a vibrant symphony of flavors working harmoniously to soothe and heal.

These anti-inflammatory juices, rich in antioxidants and anti-inflammatory agents, are more than mere beverages; they're liquid allies in your quest for wellness. Whether you're seeking relief from pain or aiming to fortify your body against inflammation, these mixtures beckon you to savor the essence of health.

Cheers to a happy, healthy, and inflammation-free you!

SINUS

Mucus, our body's defender against infections, coats the respiratory system walls and gets rid of intruders through coughing. Now, the shades of our mucus? They're like nature's code! Yellow or green might be the infection alert, while blood hints at serious business like pneumonia. And if it takes on a brownish or greyish hue, well, that's the smoking gun—literally (*Mucus congestion*, n.d.).

Surprisingly, our diet can influence mucus quality. Dairy, the sneaky culprit with its casein protein, might be thickening our mucus, especially in the nose and sinuses. So, what's the remedy? Cutting out dairy for a trial period of 1-2 weeks has been reported by some to alleviate sinus problems, despite varying opinions among doctors (*Mucus congestion*, n.d.).

Juicy fun fact: Casein is also used to make glue for things like beer bottles and wood furniture. That's how sticky it is! Imagine what it does to your nose and throat if it can glue things together! For those with allergies or asthma, mucus congestion might be a more familiar woe. The intricate interplay between respiratory health, dietary choices, and environmental factors underscores the complexity of our well-being.

One thing you could try is a juice feast with organic vegetables for 2-3 weeks. This challenge means you drink only fresh juices made from veggies like asparagus, beetroot, ginger, and carrot, or cucumber, carrot, ginger, and celery. These juices are used to help reboot your body to better cope with allergies, clear your sinuses and lungs, and give you a boost of vitamins and minerals (Patricia, 2020). Plus, they taste delicious!

Here are some recipes you could use and bid "adiós" to your sinus woes:

Hollywood Nose Job

Spinach steps into the ring like Rocky Balboa with a nutrient-packed punch! Bursting with vitamin K, iron, and folate, it's like your go to veggie for your body's essentials—from blood clotting to tissue growth. This green marvel doesn't stop there; it brings along vitamin A and lutein, offering a double dose of goodness for eye health. Spinach is your all-in-one package for nurturing your sinuses back to health.

And now, let's talk about cucumber—the hydrating virtuoso that transforms your sinuses into a moisture haven. With a supporting cast of vitamin K, magnesium, and potassium, cucumber takes the lead in promoting healthy blood circulation and nerve function. It's nothing but bliss for your sinus passages, fostering a sense of calm and balance. Not to mention its anti-inflammatory and antioxidant prowess, cucumber is on a mission to reduce swelling and tackle oxidative stress (*Mucus congestion,* n.d.). Your sinuses are in for a treat!

Serving Size:

- 16 oz

Ingredients:

- 2 inches of cucumber
- 1/4 pineapple

- 1 stalk celery
- 1 lime
- 1/4 avocado
- 2 apples
- 1/2 inch of ginger
- 10 cups of spinach leaves

Directions:

1. Wash and measure all the produce correctly.
2. Chop the spinach, celery, cucumber, and ginger into smaller parts.
3. Core and cut the apple into 4 parts.
4. Peel and cut the lime into quarters.
5. Peel and chop off the crown of the pineapple.
6. Use a spoon to remove the avocado from peel.
7. Apart from the avocado, run everything through the juicer and juice it up!
8. Run the avocado and juice through a blender at a slow pace till you have a smoothie consistency.
9. Sip and enjoy mucus free nasal passages!

Ginger Zinger Nasal Shot

If you're feeling congested, you might want to try ginger. This spicy root is not only good for making tea or adding flavor to your dishes, but it also has some amazing properties that can help you breathe easier.

Ginger is an expectorant and mucolytic, which means it can break down the sticky mucus that clogs your airways and make it easier to expel. Ginger is like a natural plumber for your lungs, clearing out the gunk and leaving you with fresh air.

If you're feeling stuffy and sneezy, you might want to mix some apples into your juice. Why? Because they contain a magical molecule called quercetin, which is like a superhero for your sinuses. Quercetin fights off the bad guys (free radicals) and calms down the drama queens (histamines) that make your nose run and your eyes water. Apples are naturally high in quercetin. So next time you have a sniffle, skip the pills and try this Ginger Zinger Nasal Shot (*Mucus congestion,* n.d.). Your nose will say "Bless you!"

Serving Size: 10 oz

Ingredients:

- 1/2 of a big apple
- 2 inches of ginger root

Directions:

1. Wash and measure the correct amount of ingredients.
2. Core the apple and cut it into quarters.
3. Chop the ginger into sections.

4. Run everything through the juicer.
5. Sip your shot and no more snot!

Balboa Nose Punch

Unleash the power of nature to clear your sinuses and boost immunity with this vibrant juice recipe! Pineapple, orange, and ginger join forces, packing a punch of vitamin C and anti-inflammatory goodness. This delightful concoction not only helps prevent and treat infections and allergies but also provides soothing relief for your cough and throat. Enjoy the delicious and healthful benefits of this easy-to-make juice, a natural remedy to invigorate your sinuses and fortify your immune system (Patricia, 2020). Sip away from a refreshing boost to your well-being!

Serving Size: about 16 oz

Ingredients:

- 2 celery sticks
- 1/4 pineapple
- a pinch of cayenne pepper
- 1 lemon
- 2 oranges
- 1 inch of ginger

Directions:

1. Wash and weigh the fruits as instructed.
2. Chop the celery and ginger into pieces.
3. Peel and cut the oranges and lemon into quarters.
4. Peel and remove the crown from the pineapple.
5. Juice the everything together and add a pinch of cayenne pepper if desired for an extra punch and flavor.
6. Enjoy your juice fresh or refrigerate for later.

Superman's Sinus Juice

Indulge in a spicy and health-packed adventure with Superman's Sinus Juice! Crafted from fresh ginger, cayenne pepper, and citrus fruits, this zesty concoction is loaded with vitamin C and anti-inflammatory goodness.

It's perfect for preventing and treating colds, allergies, and congestion, and it's also a soothing elixir for your throat and cough. Spice up your wellness routine with this easy-to-make, refreshing juice that brings a burst of natural relief to your sinuses (Patalsky, 2020).

Serving Size: about 16 oz

Ingredients:

- as much cayenne pepper as you can handle
- a pinch of salt
- 1 medium apple

- 1/2 lemon
- 1 orange
- 2 inches of fresh ginger

Directions:

1. Wash and measure all the fruits as instructed.
2. Cut the ginger onto pieces.
3. Core and cut the apple into quarters.
4. Peel and cut the orange and lemon into quarters.
5. Juice the orange, lemon, apple, and ginger together.
6. Add cayenne pepper and salt to your preference.
7. Enjoy your juice fresh or refrigerate for later.

These nose-nuzzling elixirs aren't just ordinary blends; they're your aromatic escape pods to serenity and spunk. Packed with the magic of ingredients like pineapple, orange, ginger, and a few surprises up their sleeves, these juices are like a nasal revamp and an immunity pep talk rolled into one.

Take a generous gulp, let the flavors throw a lively party in your mouth, and watch as the enchanting powers of nature play their quirky tune in your nasal passages.

COLD AND FLU

Don't let the yummy taste fool you; the following juices are more than just treats. They're loaded with the power of fresh produce, full of the nutrients your body needs to fight off colds and flu.

So, whether you want to stay healthy or just enjoy the good things in life, these recipes are your way to a delicious and nutritious adventure. Each gulp is a celebration of wellness, a splash of flavors that not only tickles your tongue but feeds your body from the inside out.

They are designed to tackle various cold and flu symptoms, boosting your immunity and enhancing your wellbeing.

Citrus Justice League

This juice is a classic combination of citrus fruits that can provide you with a lot of vitamin C and antioxidants. It can help you lower your blood pressure, cholesterol, and inflammation (Power of Positivity, 2023).

Serving Size: 18 oz

Ingredients:

- 1 grapefruit
- 4 clementines
- 1 lemon
- 2 oranges

- a pinch of salt (optional)

Directions:

1. Peel everything and cut into quarters.
2. Juice the fruits together and add salt to taste.

Juicy Infector Protector

Forget about those boring multivitamins. This juice contains the awesome foursome your body needs to fend off infections. Apples and oranges bring the C-factor, while carrots supply the A-team and the B-6 squad. Ginger is the powerful anti-inflammatory. Together, they fight off infections and make you feel awesome. Try it today and see the difference. This juice is not just good, it's super good. It's the unbeatable tag team for your health (Lokshin, 2023).

Serving Size: 20 oz

Ingredients:

- 2 inches of ginger
- 2 oranges
- 2 large carrots
- 2 apples (Granny Smith preferred)

Directions:

1. Wash the produce.
2. Chop the ginger into pieces.
3. Trim the tops of the carrots and chop them into pieces.
4. Core and cut the apple into quarters.
5. Peel and cut the orange into quarters.
6. Add everything to the juicer and juice up a storm.

Lemony Ginmeric Juice

A spicy and tangy blend of lemon and ginger that can help you improve your digestion, metabolism, and immunity. It can also help you detoxify your body and soothe your throat. Honey is an anti-bacterial and helps fight off infection (Power of Positivity, 2023).

Serving Size: 6-8 oz

Ingredients:

- 1 inch of turmeric
- 2 tablespoons of honey
- 1 inch of ginger
- juice of 2 lemons

Directions:

1. Wash the turmeric and ginger.

2. Chop the turmeric and ginger into pieces.
3. Peel and cut the lemon into quarters.
4. Add everything to the juicer and juice away.
5. Add the honey and enjoy.

Ginger Carrot Infection Beeter

Indulge in the invigorating medley of beetroot, carrot, ginger, and apple with this revitalizing juice. Beyond its delightful taste, this concoction serves as a powerhouse for enhancing blood circulation, supporting liver function, and strengthening your immune defenses. Sip your way to a healthier you, as this vibrant blend also contributes to maintaining optimal blood pressure and cholesterol levels (Lokshin, 2023). Embrace the goodness in every drop!

Serving Size: 12 oz

Ingredients:

- 1 apple
- 1 inch of ginger
- 2 carrots (large)
- 1 beetroot (medium)

Directions:

1. Wash everything thoroughly.
2. Core and slice the apple into quarters.

3. Chop off the top of the beetroot and cut into quarters.
4. Chop the ginger into parts.
5. Juice the ingredients together and enjoy.

Tomato Juicy Cold Buster

This juice is a simple but nutritious drink that can help you with your vitamin A, C, K1, B9 (folate), and potassium intake. It can also help you prevent infections and support your heart health (Lokshin, 2023).

Serving Size: 16 oz

Ingredients:

- a stalk of basil leaves
- a pinch of salt and pepper
- 4 tomatoes (medium)

Directions:

1. Wash and cut the tomatoes into quarters.
2. Juice the tomatoes and season with salt and pepper.
3. Garnish with basil leaves if desired and enjoy.

Kale and Tomato Powerhouse

This juice is a green powerhouse that can help you with your vitamin A, C, K1 intake. It can also help you detoxify your body and lower your inflammation levels (Lokshin, 2023).

Serving Size: 16 oz

Ingredients:

- 1/4 lemon
- 2 tomatoes (medium)
- salt
- 2 celery stalks
- 4 kale leaves (stemless)

Directions:

1. Wash the tomatoes, kale, and celery.
2. Chop the celery and kale into pieces.
3. Remove the lemon's peel.
4. Cut the tomato into quarters.
5. Juice the ingredients and season with salt.

Berry Bliss Fusion

Quench your thirst with the delightful fusion of sweet strawberries and tangy kiwi in this refreshing drink. Beyond its delightful taste, this concoction is a vitamin C powerhouse, offering benefits for your skin health and digestion (Lokshin, 2023). Sip and savor the goodness that nature has to offer!

Serving Size: 12 oz

Ingredients:

- 1/2 a cup of water
- 2 kiwis
- honey
- 8 strawberries

Directions:

1. Wash and hull the strawberries.
2. Peel the kiwi and cut it into halves.
3. You want to have a smoothie consistency with this one, so I would suggest using a blender instead of a juicer.
4. Blend the ingredients together until smooth and sweeten with honey.
5. Enjoy your juice fresh or refrigerate for later.

Mango Berry Tango

This juice is a tropical and delicious mix of strawberry and mango that can help you with your vitamin A, C, E, folate, and iron intake. It can also help you prevent infections and support your eye health (Lokshin, 2023).

Serving Size: 24 oz

Ingredients:

- 1 cup of water
- 1 cup of mango juice
- 1 cup of strawberry juice
- honey

Directions:

1. Wash and hull the strawberries.
2. Peel and cut the mango into chunks after removing the pit.
3. Once again, here it's better to use a blender in order to get that smoothie-like consistency.
4. Blend the ingredients together until smooth and sweeten with honey as desired.

Don't let the germs get you down this winter. Fight back with these awesome elixirs that will make your immune system stronger than ever. These drinks are loaded with nutrients, antioxidants, and anti-inflammatories that will help you ward off colds and flu like a boss. Plus, they taste amazing and will make you feel cozy and happy.

Whether you need to boost your immunity, ease your symptoms, or just enjoy a lip-smacking and healthy beverage, these preparations have got you covered.

Drink up, enjoy the flavor, and let the magic of nature protect you from the nasty bugs this winter!

DIABETES

Fresh juice can still be a delightful part of your lifestyle even with diabetes. Don't fret! There's a lineup of delicious and nutritious juice recipes tailored for those mindful of sugar levels and rich in essential vitamins and minerals.

Before we dive into the recipes, let's chat about some fruits and veggies that play nice with diabetes. We're talking about the ones with a low glycemic index, meaning they won't send your blood sugar levels on a rollercoaster ride.

Some diabetes-friendly fruits and veggies include the following examples (*4 must-try*, 2018):

- romaine
- beets
- parsley
- tomatoes
- carrots
- lemons
- garlic
- cucumbers
- ginger
- apples

- celery
- spinach
- watercress
- cabbage
- kale

Feel free to get creative with these ingredients to craft your unique juice blends, or simply try out the recipes provided below. As a friendly reminder, keep a close eye on your blood sugar levels and, before making any significant changes to your diet, it's a good idea to consult with your doctor.

Kaleidoscope Kick

In the Kaleidoscope Kick, a rich tomato base seamlessly intertwines with an ensemble of vegetables and a hint of garlic, creating a symphony of flavors that not only delights your taste buds but also delivers a kick of support for blood pressure, cholesterol, and heart health (*4 must-try*, 2018). Sip your way to a vibrant, health-infused experience!

Serving Size: 48 oz

Ingredients:

- a handful of spinach
- a handful of watercress
- 2 stalks of celery
- 3 leaves of romaine

- 2 medium carrots
- a clove of garlic
- 1 and a 1/2 beetroot
- a small bunch of parsley
- 4 medium tomatoes
- a pinch of salt

Directions:

1. Wash the beet, carrot, celery, romaine, parsley, spinach, tomato, watercress, and garlic.
2. Remove the stems and peel the outer layer of the beet.
3. Cut the carrot tops.
4. Remove the garlic skin.
5. Cut everything into pieces that fit your juicer.
6. Juice them all together and add salt to taste.

Crispy Cabbage Zest

Introducing an invigorating blend that's not just green, tangy, and crunchy but also a nutritional powerhouse. Packed with antioxidants, fiber, and chlorophyll sourced from kale and cabbage, this juice is designed to elevate your well-being. With benefits ranging from supporting weight loss to aiding digestion and fortifying your immunity, it's a refreshing experience that nourishes and energizes (Rico, 2023).

Serving Size: 24 oz

Ingredients:

- 1 lemon
- 2 leaves of chard
- 1 green apples
- 2 stalks of celery
- 1/4 of a green cabbage
- 2 leaves of kale

Directions:

1. Wash the chard, kale, cabbage, apple and celery.
2. Peel the lemon.
3. Cut everything into pieces that fit your juicer.
4. Juice them all together and enjoy!

Cucumber Lemon Mint Juice

This juice is hydrating, cooling, and soothing. It has a high water content from the cucumbers and a refreshing flavor from the lemon and mint. It also helps with skin health, detoxification, and inflammation (Rico, 2023).

Serving Size: 16 oz

Ingredients:

- a handful of mint leaves
- 1 lemon

- 2 large cucumbers

Directions:

1. Wash and peel the cucumbers and lemon.
2. Wash the mint leaves.
3. Cut all your ingredients into pieces that fit your juicer.
4. Juice them up and sip away!

Ginger Kissed Bliss

A delightful blend of sweetness, spiciness, and refreshment. Anchored by a fantastic carrot base that harmonizes with the zing of apples, the zesty kick of lemon, and the warming essence of ginger, it's a symphony for your taste buds. Beyond its deliciousness, this mixture is here to lend a hand to your digestion, blood pressure, immunity, and vision. Experience the joy of sipping on wellness with every kiss (Rico, 2023).

Serving Size: 12-16 oz

Ingredients:

- 1 inch piece of ginger
- 4 large carrots
- 2 medium apples
- 1 lemon

Directions:

1. Wash and peel the carrots, apples, lemon, and ginger.
2. Cut them into pieces that fit your juicer.
3. Run them through your juicer and juice up a storm!

The Dandelion King

A majestic blend that reigns supreme in the realm of refreshing and nutritious elixirs. This royal concoction features a harmonious mix of kale, spinach, cucumber, and green apple, crowned with the zesty influence of lemon and the earthy touch of ginger. Fit for royalty, this juice offers a verdant burst of antioxidants, vitamins, and minerals. As you sip the King of the Jungle, feel the regal embrace of wellness and vitality. Bow down to the reign of health (Rico, 2023).

Serving Size: 16 oz

Ingredients:

- 2 green apples
- 1 big bunch of dandelion leaves
- 1 lemon
- 5 celery ribs

Directions:

1. Wash the dandelion leaves, celery, and apples.
2. Peel the lemon and cut it into quarters.
3. Core and cut the apple into quarters.
4. Chop the dandelion and celery.
5. Put everything through a juicer.
6. Serve the juice fresh or refrigerate for up to 24 hours.

The Pepper Powerplay

This juice recipe is good for blood sugar control, as it contains antioxidants like lycopene, vitamin C, and beta-carotene, which help lower blood glucose levels and prevent oxidative stress. It also has spinach, celery, and kiwi, which add more vitamins, minerals, and fiber (Rico, 2023).

Serving Size: 12 oz

Ingredients:

- 1 red bell pepper
- 1 kiwi
- 2 celery sticks
- 1 bunch of spinach leaves

Directions:

1. Wash all the produce.
2. Chop the spinach, pepper, and celery.
3. Peel and cut the kiwi into quarters.
4. Run everything through a juicer.
5. Sip away!

Red Rhapsody Refresher

This juice recipe is great for heart health, as it contains tomatoes, which are rich in lycopene, a powerful antioxidant that protects against cardiovascular diseases. It also has lettuce, which adds water and fiber (Rico, 2023).

Serving Size: 16 oz

Ingredients:

- 1 bunch of lettuce
- 2 big tomatoes

Directions:

1. Wash and chop the tomatoes and lettuce.
2. Put them through a juicer.
3. Serve the juice fresh or refrigerate for up to 24 hours.

Melon Magic Infusion

This juice recipe is made from bitter melon, which is a miracle fruit that targets high blood glucose levels by increasing insulin sensitivity and reducing glucose absorption. However, it has a very bitter taste that may not appeal to everyone. You can add some other fruits or water to make it more palatable (Rico, 2023).

Serving Size: 12 oz

Ingredients:

- 2 bitter melons
- some water
- other fruits such as cucumber, green apple, or lemon

Directions:

1. Wash and chop the bitter melons (and other fruits if using).
2. Put them through a juicer.
3. Sip away and enjoy!

Potato Perfection Potion

A delightful fusion of sweet potato and green apple that creates a symphony of flavors and health benefits. This enchanting blend boasts a wealth of fiber, promoting the maintenance of balanced blood glucose levels. Sip on the sweet and refreshing essence of this elixir, satisfying your cravings with every delightful drop (Rico, 2023).

Serving Size: 12 oz

Ingredients:

- 1 inch of ginger
- 1 sweet potato
- 2 celery stalks
- cinnamon powder
- 1 green apple

Directions:

1. Wash the ginger, celery, and apple.
2. Peel the sweet potato and core the apple.
3. Chop everything into pieces that fit into your juicer.
4. Add the cinnamon powder and juice up a storm!

Brassica Blast Sip

This juice recipe is perfect for type 2 diabetics, as it contains sulforaphane, a compound that helps regulate glucose production and insulin sensitivity. It also has carrots and apples, which add sweetness and vitamin A and C (Rico, 2023).

Serving Size: 18 oz

Ingredients:

- 2 apples
- 3 carrots
- 1 broccoli head

Directions:

1. Wash and chop the broccoli.
2. Chop off the heads of the carrots.
3. Remove the cores of the apples.
4. Put them through a juicer.
5. Sip up and enjoy!

The Evergreen Elixir

A jubilant composition of chard, kale, cabbage, spinach, and celery, the virtuosos of detoxification and digestion. This harmonious blend is elevated by the sweet and tangy notes of apple and lemon, creating a symphony of flavors and health benefits (Rico, 2023).

Serving Size: 24 oz

Ingredients:

- 1 1/2 chard leaves
- 3/4 cup of kale
- 2 medium leaves of cabbage

- 1 green apple (large)
- 1 stalk of celery
- 1 lemon (medium)

Directions:

1. Wash everything and peel the lemon (cut it into quarters).
2. Cut everything into pieces that will fit into your juicer.
3. Juice everything nicely and serve fresh or refrigerate for 24 hours.

The Orchard Cleanse

This juice recipe has a healthy base of carrots, apples, lemon, and ginger, which help decrease the risk of diabetes and control sugar levels. It also has a lot of other health benefits, such as boosting immunity, digestion, and detoxification (*4 must-try*, 2018).

Serving Size: 12 oz

Ingredients:

- 1 1/3 inch of ginger
- 1 apple (medium)
- 1 lemon (medium)
- 2 carrots (large)

Directions:

1. Wash everything thoroughly.
2. Core and cut the apple into quarters.
3. Remove the carrot's head and cut it into pieces.
4. Chop the ginger.
5. Put all the ingredients through a juicer and enjoy.

In a nutshell, managing diabetes doesn't mean sacrificing the joy of enjoying delicious and nutritious juices. By choosing ingredients with a low glycemic index, you can savor a variety of flavors while keeping your blood sugar levels in check. These juice recipes for diabetics offer a refreshing and health-conscious way to incorporate essential vitamins and minerals into your diet.

Remember, it's essential to maintain a balanced approach, monitor your blood sugar levels diligently, and, as always, consult with your healthcare provider for personalized advice on dietary changes.

Cheers to a vibrant and well-balanced life!

WEIGHT LOSS

Discover the miracle of homemade green juices—a delightful journey into low-calorie refreshment. The magic lies in their minimal fruit content, ensuring a reduction in natural sugars that frees you from the worry of adding extra calories to your diet.

For those aspiring to trim down, homemade vegetable juice emerges as a staunch ally in the pursuit of fat loss goals. By swapping sugary beverages for these vibrant green elixirs, you pave the way for significant health improvements without resorting to extreme measures like juice fasts (Forrest, 2021).

In a league of their own, these green wonders outshine other beverages, especially those laced with added sugars like sodas. The latter tends to send your blood sugar levels on a rollercoaster ride, triggering insatiable cravings for sweets. Homemade green juices, on the other hand, serve as a wise and delicious alternative, helping you sidestep these pitfalls and fortify your weight loss endeavors.

Hydration takes center stage in the benefits of homemade green juices. Beyond quenching your thirst, these nutrient-dense creations supply your body with essential electrolytes and nutrients, fostering a sense of vitality and nourishment. Satisfying your sweet cravings, they tantalize your taste buds with fresh and natural flavors, making the journey to health a flavorful and enjoyable one.

Real-Life Testimonial: Green Thickies

Meet Katherine Kyle, the mastermind behind the "Green Thickies" weight loss juice and the author of *7 Day Detox. 7 Days to a Total Body Transformation* (Kyle, 2019). Katherine battled with being overweight for the majority of her life, experimenting with various diets that failed to yield results. She constantly grappled with feelings of hunger, fatigue, and frustration due to her lack of progress, compounded by several health issues that left her feeling miserable.

Driven by a desire to prioritize her health and discover a natural approach to heal her body and shed excess weight, Katherine stumbled upon a book that unraveled the secrets of crafting filling green smoothies capable of replacing entire meals. Intrigued by the potential benefits of incorporating fruits, vegetables, healthy fats, and protein into her diet, she embarked on the seven-day detox for weight loss and improved health with unwavering commitment.

The results were nothing short of astonishing. In just one week, Katherine experienced a significant weight loss, accompanied by heightened energy levels, mental clarity, and an overwhelming sense of happiness. She reveled in the diverse flavors and variety offered by the green smoothies, never once experiencing feelings of hunger or deprivation.

Maintaining this newfound lifestyle, Katherine continued to incorporate green smoothies into her breakfast and lunch routines, complemented by healthy vegan dinners and increased physical activity. Within six months, she achieved a remarkable weight loss of 56 pounds, reaching her ideal weight and undergoing a profound transformation.

Pregnancy brought about new challenges as Katherine gained considerable weight, succumbing to cravings for rich and comforting foods. After giving birth, she sought to reclaim her healthy habits and turned once again to the positive experience of green smoothies. This time, recognizing the need for more filling and satisfying options, she birthed the concept of Green Thickies—complete meal green smoothies enriched with ingredients like oats, nuts, seeds, or avocados.

Perfectly suited for her role as a busy mom, Green Thickies became Katherine's go-to solution—easy to make, delicious, and nutritious, keeping her energized for extended periods. These satisfying concoctions helped her control cravings and achieve healthy weight loss.

With a Green Thickie for breakfast and another for lunch every day, complemented by a balanced vegan dinner at night, Katherine shed all of the baby weight (42 pounds) in just four months. Green Thickies not only transformed her life by improving her health and aiding in weight loss but also became an integral part of her lifestyle that she can't envision living without.

Katherine enthusiastically recommends Green Thickies to anyone seeking a tasty and healthy approach to shedding those unwanted pounds and enhance their holistic wellness.

Fruit Love-Handles Liquidator Juice

Indulge in a delightful juice crafted from a medley of ingredients. Beyond its tasteful appeal, this juice is an effective energy booster. Apples, renowned for their low-calorie, high-fiber attributes, make a valuable addition to recipes promoting weight loss. Notably, they contribute to an 86% water content, enhancing overall hydration and nutritional value (Brohl, 2020).

Serving Size: 16 oz

Ingredients:

- 1/2 a pineapple
- 2 nectarines
- 2 kiwifruits
- 2 apples

Directions:

1. Wash, core, and cut the apples into quarters.
2. Chop the green crown, peel the pineapple, and slice it into chunks.
3. Peel the nectarines and kiwis (cut into quarters).
4. Juice the nectarines and remove the seeds.
5. Combine all fruits and run through a juicer.
6. Enjoy fresh or refrigerate for 24 hours.

Apple Adipose Annihilator Juice

Kickstart your day with a nutritious breakfast juice blending the goodness of low calories. Spinach, packed with fiber vitamins A and K, pairs seamlessly with the antioxidant-rich apples. A touch of lemon adds a zesty twist, enhancing both flavor and nutritional content (Brohl, 2020).

Serving Size: 12 oz

Ingredients:

- 1 lemon
- 1 apple
- 3 handfuls of spinach

Directions:

1. Wash the apple and spinach.
2. Peel and cut the lemon into quarters.
3. Core and cut the apple into quarters.
4. Chop the spinach into pieces.
5. Run everything through a juicer and savor this nutritious breakfast blend immediately.

Green Belt Buster

Embrace the health benefits and weight loss potential of these ingredients. High water content in cucumbers, lettuce, and celery supports digestion, promoting efficient movement through the digestive tract (Brohl, 2020).

Serving Size: 18 oz

Ingredients:

- 1 small lime
- 1 handful lettuce
- 1 handful spinach
- 1 stalk celery
- 1 cucumber
- 3 apples

Directions:

1. Wash all the ingredients thoroughly.
2. Core and cut the apples into quarters.
3. Peel and cut the cucumbers into pieces.
4. Chop the celery, lettuce, and spinach into pieces.
5. Peel cucumbers and apples before juicing.
6. Run everything through a juicer and sip away!

Kale and Ginger Flab Fighter

Indulge in the anti-obesity effects and digestive health properties of kale, a leafy green powerhouse bursting with vitamins and minerals. Paired tastefully with the zingy essence of ginger root, this juice isn't just a drink; it's a vibrant symphony of health and flavor (Brohl, 2020).

Serving Size: 22 oz

Ingredients:

- 1/2 an apple
- 3 stalks celery
- an inch of ginger
- 1 cucumber
- 1 lemon
- 2 kale leaves

Directions:

1. Wash everything thoroughly.
2. Core and cut the apple into quarters.
3. Chop the ginger into pieces.
4. Peel and cut the lemon and cucumber into pieces.
5. Chop the celery and kale into pieces.
6. Run everything through a juicer and savor the nutritious blend of kale and ginger.

Carrot Coriander Chub-Charm Chug

Experience the weight loss and anti-inflammatory benefits with a carrot juice masterpiece. Packed with the essential nutrients from carrots, cucumber, and coriander, and featuring a refreshing twist of lemon and ginger, this concoction isn't just a drink, it's a sip of health and flavor combined (Brohl, 2020).

JADE JUICE

Serving Size: 18 oz

Ingredients:

- an inch of ginger
- 3 carrots
- 1 cucumber
- 1 teaspoon lemon juice
- 2 handfuls coriander

Directions:

1. Wash all the produce thoroughly.
2. Chop the heads off the carrots and into smaller pieces.
3. Chop cucumber into smaller pieces.
4. Chop the coriander into smaller pieces.
5. Pour lemon juice into the glass before running all the other ingredients through the juicer.
6. Enjoy this revitalizing weight loss wonder!

Tangy Broc Slimdown

Support weight loss and fortify your immune system with a juice comprising broccoli, carrot, and celery. This dynamic trio not only promises a flavorful experience but also serves as your ticket to a healthier, more vibrant you. This "Biggest Loser" combination offers essential minerals and vitamins while being low in calories and high in fiber (Brohl, 2020).

Serving Size: 18 oz

Ingredients:

- 1 stalk of celery
- 1 carrot
- 2 oranges
- 2 cups of broccoli

Directions:

1. Wash all your ingredients thoroughly.
2. Chop the head of the carrot off.
3. Peel and cut the orange into quarters.
4. Chop broccoli, carrot, and celery into chunks that will fit into your juicer.
5. Juice everything together and delight in the nutrient-rich—low-calorie juice.

Watermelon Waistline Whiz

Quench your thirst with a soda alternative that's as refreshing as it is healthy—watermelon juice. Packed with almost 100 percent water content, watermelons aren't just hydrating; they're your ticket to better digestion, glowing skin, and reduced blood pressure levels. Say *au revoir* to soda and hello to a sip that's pure, juicy goodness (Brohl, 2020).

Serving Size: 12 oz

Ingredients:

- a small handful of mint leaves
- 1 small lemon
- 3 cups of diced watermelon

Directions:

1. Wash the mint leaves.
2. Peel and cut the lemon into quarters.
3. Slice the watermelons into chunks.
4. Run everything through a juicer, including the watermelon rind.

Cauli-Fruit Slimdown Juice

Spoil yourself with a nutrient-packed fusion with this juice boasting the goodness of cauliflower, carrots, beets, and apples. Did you know cauliflower is as hydrating as watermelon? Beyond that, it's your memory's best friend, your circulation's cheerleader, and your bones' trusted ally. Get ready for a sip that's not just a treat for your taste buds but a wellness wonder for your body (Brohl, 2020).

Serving Size: 16 oz

Ingredients:

- 2 apples

- 1 cup cauliflower
- 1 beet
- 2 carrots

Directions:

1. Wash everything thoroughly.
2. Core and cut the apples into quarters.
3. Cut the tops off the carrots and the beets (peel the skin), and cut them into pieces.
4. Chop cauliflower into smaller pieces.
5. Juice everything together and enjoy!

Beet & Blackberry Infusion Juice

Find harmony in a symphony of flavors with this vibrant juice concoction. It's not just a sip, it's a delightful dance of ingredients designed to not only support your weight loss journey but also give your heart a nutritional hug. Get ready for a taste explosion that's as satisfying as it is nutritious (Brohl, 2020).

Serving Size: 24 oz

Ingredients:

- 1 inch piece of ginger
- 1 cup blackberries
- 3 medium-sized beets
- 2 apples

Directions:

1. Wash the blackberries and beets (chop off the tops).
2. Core and chop the apples into quarters.
3. Slice the beets into chunks.
4. Juice all ingredients for a delicious and nutritious blend.

Savor a symphony of flavors and bask in the nutritional richness of these juice recipes, tailor-made to accompany you on your weight loss journey. Integrate them seamlessly into a well-rounded diet for optimal and delightful results. Revel in the delicious taste while your body absorbs the goodness of essential vitamins and minerals.

Cheers to a flavorful and nourishing approach to your wellness!

PRE- AND POST-WORKOUT

Fueling up with the right energy is key to unlocking your full workout potential. And what better way to do it than indulging in the goodness served up by a juicer? In reality, our bodies crave that energy boost, especially when gearing up for an intense session, be it cardio or weightlifting. It's high time we debunk the myth that having a bite or a sip before a workout is a no-go. It's not just a win-win; it's a delicious prelude to a highly effective workout.

Tackling a gym session with a healthy glass of juice offers a myriad of benefits (*Juicing recipes,* n.d.):

1. Initiates cellular repair, curbing inflammation resulting from physical stress.
2. Elevates respiratory function, paving the way for enhanced endurance training.
3. Acts as a powerful antioxidant, combating oxidative stress triggered by rigorous exercises.

Similarly, replenishing your body post-workout deserves a touch of freshness, and homemade juice stands out as a superior choice over your regular cup of coffee. Many fitness coaches and trainers will agree that opting for a hydrating green juice is the ultimate strategy to infuse your body with live enzymes, vitamins, and essential nutrients after a vigorous workout (Proudfoot, 2015).

Ditch the store-bought sports drinks laden with unhealthy processed sugars and make a wise switch to a revitalizing homemade juice. Not only does it steer clear of detrimental additives, but it also ensures optimal hydration, allowing you to make the most of your workout sessions.

To help you reach your fitness objectives and conquer the day, we've curated highly effective juice recipes. Packed with nutrients, superfoods, and wholesome goodness, these recipes are tailored to elevate both your fitness journey and your daily vitality.

Carrot Power Surge Juice

Loaded with beta-carotene, this juice does wonders by oxygenating your blood, body, and brain tissues. It boasts antioxidant properties, shielding your cells from damage. Additionally, it contains ginseng powder, providing a powerful boost in energy, stamina, and strength for your workout (*Juicing recipes,* n.d.).

Serving Size: 10 oz

Ingredients:

- 1 tablespoon of ginseng powder
- 2 inches of ginger
- 1 cup of freshly pressed carrot juice

Directions:

1. **Carrot extraction and ginger fusion:** Use a juicer to extract 1 cup of fresh carrot and ginger juice. Ensure the carrots (remove the heads) and ginger are properly washed and prepared.
2. **Power of ginseng:** Add the ginger and carrot juice and incorporate 1 tablespoon of ginseng powder.
3. **Mix it up:** Blend or stir the mixture thoroughly to ensure an even distribution of flavors.

Enjoy! Savor the nutritional goodness of this carrot juice, providing a powerful pre-workout kick for your energy needs.

Gingergetic Beet Bliss

Enhance your blood circulation with this rejuvenating beetroot, carrot, and ginger juice. Packed with nutrients that promote improved circulation and oxygen delivery, this vibrant drink is simple to prepare (*Juicing recipes,* n.d.).

Serving Size: 12 oz

Ingredients:

- 3 medium beets
- 2 carrots
- 3 inches of ginger

Directions:

- **Prepare the beets:** Peel the beets and cut them into manageable 1-inch pieces.
- **Handle the carrots:** Wash the carrots thoroughly and cut them into similar 1-inch pieces.
- **Ginger magic:** Peel the ginger and chop it into 1-inch pieces for effective juicing.
- **Juicing symphony:** Feed the prepared beets, carrots, and ginger into your juicer.

- **Strain for purity:** Pass the extracted juice through a fine-mesh sieve into a large bowl. This ensures a smooth and pulp-free consistency.

Enjoy! Your rejuvenating beetroot, carrot, and ginger juice is ready to enhance your blood circulation and invigorate your senses!

The Ultimate Warrior's Beverage

This juice is a powerhouse of phytonutrients, fighting inflammation and boosting your immune system. Apples, a key component, enhance exercise endurance by increasing oxygen availability to your lungs. It features spinach, triggering greater muscle contraction by releasing more calcium. Romaine lettuce steps in to amp up iron absorption and oxygen-carrying capacity. Cilantro contributes by cleansing your body of toxic metals. Finally, ginger and mint tag team to alleviate pain and stiffness before and after your workout (*Juicing recipes,* n.d.).

Serving Size: 20 oz

Ingredients:

- a handful of mint leaves
- a bunch of romaine lettuce
- 1 lemon
- 3 or 4 leaves of spinach or kale leaves
- a handful of fresh cilantro

- 2 apples (medium)
- 2 inches of ginger

Directions:

- **Prepare the apples:** Wash and core the green apples, then chop them into smaller pieces for easy juicing.
- **Prep the leafy greens:** If using kale, remove the tough stems. For spinach, a quick rinse will do. Tear or chop them into manageable portions.
- **Handle the romaine lettuce:** Clean the Romaine lettuce thoroughly, separating the leaves.
- **Cilantro magic:** Wash the cilantro, ensuring it's free of debris.
- **Lemon quarter:** Cut the lemon into quarters, ensuring the seeds are removed.
- **Ginger (optional):** If using ginger, peel and slice it into smaller pieces for effective juicing.
- **Minty touch:** Pick a few leaves of mint for that refreshing flavor.
- **Masticating juicer magic:** Feed all the prepared ingredients into a masticating juicer. This step ensures efficient extraction of juice while preserving maximum nutrients.
- **Adjust the flavor:** Squeeze a bit of lemon juice into the mix to fine-tune the taste according to your preference.

Juicy Hydration Oasis

Feeling post-workout parched? This juice is here to drench your thirst in the most exotic and rejuvenating way possible. With the zing of grapefruit, the tropical hug of coconut water, and a pinch of Himalayan crystal salt for that extra flair, this post-sweat elixir is your ticket to a hydration paradise (Proudfoot, 2015).

Serving Size: 12 oz

Ingredients:

- Himalayan crystal salt
- 1 cup coconut water
- 1 grapefruit

Directions:

1. Peel and chop the grapefruit.
2. Add the grapefruit, coconut water, and Himalayan crystal salt (to taste) to a juicer.
3. Juice until well combined, and enjoy!

Aurora Green Awakening

Rise and shine, workout warrior! The Aurora Green Awakening juice is your post-exercise wake-up call. Packed with the hydrating goodness of watermelon, the cool cucumber vibes, a zesty lemon kick, and a touch of ginger to rev up your senses, this green concoction is your secret weapon to post-gym revitalization (Proudfoot, 2015).

Serving Size: 12 oz

Ingredients:

- 1 inch piece of fresh ginger
- 1 cucumber
- 1/4 watermelon
- 1 lemon

Directions:

1. Quarter the watermelon for easy juicing.
2. Peel and cut the cucumber into chunks.
3. Peel the lemon to reveal its zest.
4. Add watermelon, cucumber, lemon, and ginger to a juicer.
5. Juice away and enjoy!

Kale Kickstarter

Say cheers to a post-workout detox that's as entertaining as it is cleansing. The Kale Kickstarter juice, the spicy superstar in the juice world, is here to kick back and relax your system. Kale, carrots, radishes, and a splash of citrusy goodness (Proudfoot, 2015).

JADE JUICE

Serving Size: 40 oz

Ingredients:

- 1/2 inch piece of turmeric
- 1 large apple
- 1 orange
- 1/2 inch piece of ginger
- 2 stalks celery
- 6 radishes
- 1 lemon
- 3 medium carrots

Directions:

1. Wash and cut the carrots, radishes, apple, celery, orange, lemon, ginger, and turmeric.
2. Juice or blend until smooth.
3. Strain if using a blender.

Sunburst Revitalizer Juice

Post-workout pick-me-up, anyone? Sunburst Revitalizer Juice is your instant hydrator and blood sugar balancer. With apples, pears, celery sticks, and a peppering of radishes, this juice is the cool breeze your cells need after a sweaty session. Sip, chill, and rejuvenate (Proudfoot, 2015).

Serving Size: 18 oz

Ingredients:

- 2 apples
- 2 pears
- 3 celery sticks
- 10 radishes

Directions:

1. Core and prep the apples.
2. Slice the pears.
3. Wash and cut the celery sticks.
4. Juice the apples, pears, celery sticks, and radishes.
5. Chill before drinking.

Superhuman Quencher

Calling all post-workout superhumans! Superhuman Quencher is the green potion you didn't know you needed. Celery, cucumber, spinach, wheatgrass, and a citrusy twist—it's the ultimate blend to nourish your cells and alkalize your inner superhuman (Proudfoot, 2015). Sip, conquer, repeat!

Serving Size: 16 oz

Ingredients:

- 2 celery stalks

- 1 cucumber
- 1 handful of spinach leaves
- 1 shot of wheatgrass or wheatgrass powder
- 1 orange
- 1 small handful of ice

Directions:

1. Wash and chop the celery stalks.
2. Prepare the cucumber for juicing.
3. Wash the spinach leaves.
4. Juice the celery, cucumber, and spinach.
5. Add the wheatgrass or wheatgrass powder.
6. Pour the juice over ice.

- **Pro tip:** Bite into an orange slice after each sip.

Whether you're prepping for a workout that'll make you sweat glitter or recharging those energy reserves post-gym escapades, it's all about giving your body the VIP treatment with the right nutrients. These pre- and post-workout recipes aren't just flavor gurus; they're like your personal cheer squad for your fitness odyssey. Take a sip, indulge in the goodness, and let each drop be a high-five to your wellness journey, turning your routine into a colorful fiesta.

Cheers to a spicier, zestier version of you!

CONCLUSION

Beginner's Guide to Juicing is a guide that squeezes out the secrets of juicing, making it easy-peasy for anyone, no matter their fitness level. The main squeeze is the amazing potential of juicing to boost your well-being. Let's explore the key ideas and success stories that make this book a must-read.

This guide is a complete juice map that takes you from a newbie to a pro. *Beginner's Guide to Juicing* shows you that juicing is not just a fad but a fab lifestyle choice. It gives you handy tips and tested tricks that help you start, stick to, and savor the benefits of juicing. The adventure starts with learning the basics of juicing—picking the right ingredients. From colorful fruits to nourishing veggies, the book helps you make smart choices.

It reveals the nutritional facts of various ingredients, letting you customize your juices to fit your health goals.

A key message is that juicing is for everyone. Whether you're a fitness aficionado or a wellness wizard, juicing is your friend. The book busts the myth that juicing is only for experts and shares inspiring success stories that prove this point.

Like many busy bees out there with demanding jobs—I lived a lifestyle that often left me feeling zapped and sleepy. Struggling with low energy levels, I depended on coffee and candy to get through my days. That changed when I discovered the magic of juicing. My journey with juicing began cautiously, as I was not sure about the hype. But, driven by a wish to regain my zest, I began adding fresh, nutrient-rich juices to my daily routine.

The results were nothing short of amazing. I made sure this book includes practical insights into making the perfect juice blends. It tackles common problems and offers solutions for those times when things go wrong. Through fun stories and realistic situations, the book makes sure you feel backed up in your juicing efforts.

A special feature of *Beginner's Guide to Juicing* is its focus on personalization. The book knows that different strokes work for different folks when it comes to juicing. Readers are urged to try out different flavors, textures, and combos to find what tickles their taste buds and meets their nutritional needs. But the book goes beyond just the physical perks of juicing; it also looks at the mental and emotional sides.

Juicing is seen not just as a food choice or diet but as a way of life and caring for yourself. It digs into the mindfulness of juicing—being conscious in the process of choosing, making, and enjoying each sip. I've made sure to add a sprinkle of tips on how to fit juicing into busy schedules. One of my aims is to shatter the myth that juicing is time-wasting and unrealistic for those with hectic lives.

Instead, my book promotes juicing as a time-saving and doable habit. The success stories in this book serve as sources of inspiration. Readers see real people achieving real results through juicing. Whether it's losing weight, beating health issues, or just feeling livelier, these stories confirm the power of juicing.

My journey with juicing not only rocked my overall health but also cleared up my stubborn skin issues. I battled with various skin woes for years, trying different skincare routines and treatments without finding a lasting solution. It was only when I embraced juicing that I found a natural way to heal my skin from within. I started adding a variety of fruits and vegetables known for their skin-boosting properties to my daily juices.

Antioxidant-packed berries, refreshing cucumber, and cleansing greens became must-haves in my blends. The impact was astonishing—my skin started to glow with the nourishment I was giving it from the inside, shining with new radiance. My success story is a powerful example of how juicing can be a great sidekick in combating skin villains. By feeding my body with the right mix of ingredients, I not only solved specific skin problems but also improved my overall health and confidence.

If you've struggled with pesky health issues, consider my journey as a motivating story. Juicing might just be the secret ingredient in your healthcare routine, offering a natural and wholesome way to achieve your much sought-after healing.

As I wrap up this book, I'd like to nudge you toward action. The ball is in your court to start your juicing journey, armed with the knowledge and inspiration from the book. I promise you that you don't need a fitness background to start—just the curiosity to try something new.

Please feel free to share your experiences and reviews, creating a community of people who love juicing and well-being. In a nutshell, *Beginner's Guide to Juicing* is not just a guide; it's an invitation to transform your life. It celebrates the fun and joy of juicing while recognizing its awesome impact on health.

As you turn the final page, you're not just loaded with knowledge; you're fired up with the inspiration to make juicing a lasting and rewarding part of your journey to vibrant health. So, are you ready to unleash the power of juicing in your life?

The adventure awaits—grab your copy, start juicing, and share your success story. Your journey is unique, and your story can inspire others to start their own path to wellness.

My final message is this: Juicing is not a fad but a cool and enjoyable lifestyle choice.

Cheers to a vibrant, juiced-up life!

Your Juicy Journey Matters!

Hey there, super juicer!

Guess what? You've just zoomed through "Change The Way You Feel: Juicing For Beginners"! Now you're all geared up with awesome tips and tricks to boost your energy, enjoy better sleep, sharpen your focus, and kick-start a healthier life. Pretty cool, right?

But wait, your juicy journey doesn't end here. It's time to pass the baton and light the way for others who are just starting out. How? By sharing your honest thoughts about this book on Amazon!

Your review is like a guiding star for others who are searching for the same vibrant health and happiness that you've discovered. By leaving your review, you're not just saying what you think; you're showing others where to find their path to a healthier, happier life.

So, why keep all this juicy goodness to yourself? Spread the love! Your words can inspire, encourage, and guide someone else on their journey to a better life. It's all about sharing the joy and benefits of juicing with the world.

Thank you so much for being a part of this. The world of juicing stays alive and kicking when we share our experiences – and you're playing a big part in that.

Ready to make a difference? Scan the QR Code to leave your review on Amazon and help light the way for a fellow juice enthusiast.

Your thoughts matter more than you know, and I can't thank you enough for sharing them.

Juice on!

Jade Juice

REFERENCES

10 best detox juice recipes for weight loss. Insanely Good Recipes. (2022, October 10). https://insanelygoodrecipes.com/detox-juice-recipes/

11 energizing juice recipes to kickstart your day. Hurom. (n.d.). https://www.hurom.com/pages/11-energizing-juice-recipes-to-kick-start-your-day

3-Day DIY juice cleanse (recipes, benefits & tips). Goodnature. (2023, March 8). https://www.goodnature.com/blog/3-day-diy-juice-cleanse

4 must-try juice recipes for diabetics. Goodnature. (2018, June 1). https://www.goodnature.com/blog/4-great-juice-recipes-for-diabetics

5-day cleanse: What to expect. Pressed. (n.d.). https://pressed.com/blog/5-day-cleanse-what-to-expect

5-Day juice plan - lakeland. (2013). https://www.lakeland.co.uk/content/documents/5-Day-Plan_Updated.pdf

Ali, R. (2019, February 15). *Beyonce lost 20 pounds with a juice cleanse. here are the pros and cons of the crash detox*. USA Today. https://www.usatoday.com/story/life/2019/02/15/juice-cleanse-pros-cons-juice-detox-beyonce-lemonade-diet-master-cleanse/2811373002/

Beiser, A. (2023, February 24). *The 10 best detox juice recipes*. GypsyPlate. https://gypsyplate.com/the-best-detox-juice-recipes/

Blackwood, M. (2023, March 8). *10 benefits of juicing*. Healthier Steps. https://healthiersteps.com/10-amazing-benefits-of-juicing-raw-fruits-and-vegetables/

Brohl, P. (2020, July 25). *22 healthy juicing recipes for weight loss*. Vibrant Happy Healthy. https://vibranthappyhealthy.com/weight-loss-juice-recipes

Brown, M. J. (2019, October 4). *Juicing: Good or bad?*. Healthline. https://www.healthline.com/nutrition/juicing-good-or-bad

REFERENCES

Case studies. Juiceology. (n.d.). https://www.juice-ology.co.uk/case-studies

Cassani, V. (2022, October 17). *Beginner's Guide to Juicing : Everything You Need to get started!* Live Simply Natural. https://livesimplynatural.com/beginners-guide-juicing/

Cole, W. (2023, June 26). *Best juicing recipes to reduce inflammation.* Dr. Will Cole. https://drwillcole.com/functional-medicine/the-best-juice-recipes-to-fight-inflammation

Delgado, J. (2023, September 25). ▷ *what are expectations? its psychological meaning.* Psychology Spot. https://psychology-spot.com/expectations-examples-meaning/

Ding, S. (2019, March 25). *Juice fasting - the complete guide on What you need to know.* Juicing For Health. https://juicing-for-health.com/juice-fasting

Eatough, E. (2023, May 8). *How to set goals and achieve them: 10 strategies for Success.* BetterUp. https://www.betterup.com/blog/how-to-set-goals-and-achieve-them

Emily. (2022, December 9). Is juicing non-organic fruits and vegetables safe? - simply Healthy Vegan. https://simplyhealthyvegan.com/is-juicing-non-organic-fruits-and-vegetables-safe/

Forrest, C. (2021, October 7). *10+ best juice recipes for weight loss.* Clean Eating Kitchen. https://www.cleaneatingkitchen.com/juice-recipes-for-weight-loss/

Frey, R. (2020, February 25). *11 creative ways to use leftover Juice Pulp.* Goodnature. https://www.goodnature.com/blog/11-creative-ways-to-use-leftover-juice-pulp

Frey, R. (2021, January 25). *How to store produce for juice.* Goodnature. https://www.goodnature.com/blog/how-to-store-produce-for-juice

Frey, R. (2023, April 20). *7 juice recipes for Gut Health & Inflammation.* Goodnature. https://www.goodnature.com/recipes/juicing-for-gut-health-inflammation

Galea, T. (2023, June 3). *List of essential juicing tools – a guide to juicing for Beginners.* Juicing With Tania. https://www.juicingwithtania.com/blog/list-of-essential-juicing-tools/

REFERENCES | 203

Georgiou, C. (2015, August 5). *Juicing for improved energy*. Joe Cross. https://www.rebootwithjoe.com/juicing-for-improved-energy/

Georgiou, Claire. (2018, March 15). *A juice to help clear your sinuses*. Joe Cross. https://www.rebootwithjoe.com/a-juice-to-help-clear-your-sinuses/

Good Food Is Good Medicine. (2019, April 5). *Are Organic Foods really healthier? Two pediatricians break it down*. good-food. https://health.ucdavis.edu/blog/good-food/are-organic-foods-really-healthier-two-pediatricians-break-it-down/2019/04

Henning, S. M. (2017, May 19). *Health benefit of vegetable/fruit juice-based diet: Role of microbiome*. Scientific reports. https://www.ncbi.nlm.nih.gov/pmc/articles/PMC5438379/

Juicing recipes to try before hitting the gym. Energise Your Life. (n.d.). https://www.energiseyourlife.com/blog/juicing-recipes-to-try-before-hitting-the-gym/

Kennedy, S. (2022, April 27). *The top 11 juicing myths busted*. Joe Cross. https://www.rebootwithjoe.com/juicing-myths/

Kyle, K. (2019, September 19). *How I lost 56 pounds with the green smoothie diet and Green Thickies*. Green Thickies: Filling Green Smoothie Recipes. https://www.greenthickies.com/lost-56-pounds-green-smoothie-diet/

Leach, S. (2018, March 15). *How to start juicing: Goal setting and guidance*. Juicing and Plant Based Diet Health Coach Stephanie Leach. https://stephanieleach.com/2018/03/15/how-to-start-juicing-goal-setting-and-guidance/

Lokshin, E. (2023, March 8). *10 tasty beverages to boost your immune system*. Healthline. https://www.healthline.com/health/juice-immune-system-boost

MacPherson, R. (2022, November 4). *What is a juice cleanse?*. Verywell Fit. https://www.verywellfit.com/juice-cleanse-89120

Mayo Clinic Staff. (2022, April 22). *Are Organic Foods Worth the price?*. Mayo Clinic. https://www.mayoclinic.org/healthy-lifestyle/nutrition-and-healthy-eating/in-depth/organic-food/art-20043880

Mucus congestion. Juice Master. (n.d.). https://www.juicemaster.com/a-z-of-ailments/mucus-congestion

Patalsky, K. (2020, March 14). *Super sinus juice recipe: Juicing for health series*. HealthyHappyLife.com - Vegan recipes and life stories with Kathy Patalsky. https://healthyhappylife.com/super-sinus-juice-juicing-for-health/

Patricia. (2020, February 27). *5 ways to keep your sinuses healthy: Sinus doctor Detroit*. Detroit Sinus Center. https://www.detroitsinuscenter.com/blog/sinus-doctor-detroit/5-ways-keep-sinuses-healthy/

Power of Positivity. (2023, May 21). *18 healthy juice recipes that make your immune system stronger*. Power of Positivity: Positive Thinking & Attitude. https://www.powerofpositivity.com/juice-recipes-make-immune-system-stronger/

Proudfoot, J. (2015, August 21). 10 best juice recipes for after exercise - red online. https://www.redonline.co.uk/wellbeing/health/a519859/10-best-juice-recipes-for-after-your-workout/

Revis, B. (2019, November 20). *Seven tips to shop organic on a budget*. Ward's Supermarket. https://wardsgainesville.com/7-tips-shop-organic-on-budget/

Rico, T. (2023, July 21). *10 effective juicing recipes for diabetics that give actual results*. PUREVEGE. https://purevege.com/best-juicing-recipes-for-diabetics/

Schaefer, A. (2018, December 4). *Juicing vs. blending: Which is better for losing weight?*. Healthline. https://www.healthline.com/health/food-nutrition/juicing-vs-blending

Sexner, A. (2015, May 15). *How to prepare produce for juice*. Goodnature. https://www.goodnature.com/blog/preparing-produce-juice

Simkins, V. (n.d.). *Best fruits and vegetables for juicing*. about. https://www.all-about-juicing.com/best-fruits-and-vegetables.html

Stathis, J. (2023, February 24). *I did a 3-day juice cleanse-here's what happened*. The Healthy. https://www.thehealthy.com/food/juice-cleanse-three-days-heres-what-happened/

Success stories. Joe Cross. (2021, June 30). https://www.rebootwithjoe.com/reboot-success-stories/

TeamReboot. (2022, June 20). *Top 10 fruits & veggies to juice right now*. Joe Cross. https://www.rebootwithjoe.com/top-10-fruits-veggies-to-juice-right-now/

Tips for storing juice. Nama. (n.d.). https://namawell.com/en-za/blogs/guide-to-juicing/tips-for-storing-juice

Walsh, G. (2021, February 15). *7 Day detox plan to kick-start your metabolism and help you lose weight.* GoodTo. https://www.goodto.com/wellbeing/7-day-detox-plan-59890

Printed in Great Britain
by Amazon